FRENCH GRAMMAR
Your Guide
Third edition

Val Levick
Glenise Radford
Alasdair McKeane

CONTENTS

Grammatical Terms explained .... Page 1

Adjectives
- Agreement .... Page 6
- Position in the sentence .... Page 9
- Comparison of adjectives .... Page 11
- Possessive adjectives .... Page 13
- Demonstrative adjectives .... Page 14
- Interrogative adjectives..................... Page 14
- Indefinite adjectives........................... Page 15

Adverbs
- Formation of adverbs......................... Page 16
- Position of adverbs .... Page 17
- Comparison of adverbs .... Page 18
- More adverbs .... Page 19

Articles
- The definite article............................. Page 20
- The indefinite article.......................... Page 21
- The partitive article............................ Page 22

Conjunctions .... Page 24

Nouns
- Gender problems................................. Page 25
- Gender endings................................... Page 26
- Masculine and feminine forms .... Page 27
- Plural of nouns.................................... Page 29
- Compound nouns................................ Page 30
- Collective nouns .... Page 31

Numbers, Dates and Time
- Cardinal numbers................................ Page 32
- Ordinal numbers .... Page 33
- Time.. Page 33
- Days of the week .... Page 34
- Months of the year............................. Page 34
- Dates .... Page 34

Prepositions .... Page 36

Contents — French Grammar

Pronouns
- Subject pronouns .... Page 41
- Object pronouns .... Page 42
- Position of pronouns .... Page 43
- Order of pronouns .... Page 44
- Emphatic pronouns .... Page 44
- Relative pronouns .... Page 45
- Interrogative pronouns .... Page 47
- Demonstrative pronouns .... Page 48
- Possessive pronouns .... Page 49
- Indefinite pronouns .... Page 50

Verbs
- Present tense .... Page 51
  - -er verbs .... Page 51
  - irregular -er verbs .... Page 52
  - -ir verbs .... Page 54
  - -re verbs .... Page 55
  - -oir verbs .... Page 56
  - reflexive verbs .... Page 56
  - special constructions .... Page 57
- Perfect tense:
  - verbs with avoir .... Page 58
  - PDO .... Page 60
  - verbs with être .... Page 60
  - reflexive verbs .... Page 61
  - perfect infinitive .... Page 62
- Imperfect tense .... Page 63
- Pluperfect tense .... Page 65
- Present participle .... Page 66
- Future tense .... Page 68
- Conditional tense .... Page 70
- Past historic .... Page 71
- The passive .... Page 74
- Imperatives .... Page 75
- Negatives .... Page 76
- Questions .... Page 79
- Modal verbs .... Page 80
- The Infinitive and its constructions ... Page 82
- Other special constructions .... Page 85
- Word order .... Page 87

Verb Table
- Regular verbs .... Page 88
- Irregular verbs .... Page 89

Index .... Page 107

GRAMMATICAL TERMS EXPLAINED

Grammatical terms are frequently thought of as boring and/or confusing, but, in reality, they need be neither. Once you have sorted out in your mind what they mean and what they do, you will realise that they are helpful, user-friendly tools for you to use in your language learning.
In this list you will find, arranged in alphabetical order, some of the terms you are likely to meet.

ADJECTIVES (LES ADJECTIFS)

These are words which describe or tell you more about a noun.
There are many kinds of adjectives: *big, blue, intelligent, French,* but they all serve to give extra information about their noun.

ADVERBS (LES ADVERBES)

These are words which are added to a verb, adjective or another adverb to tell you how *(quickly)*, when *(soon)*, where *(there)* a thing was done.

Two "technical terms" you will encounter with both adjectives and adverbs are **Comparative (Comparatif)** and **Superlative (Superlatif)**.

> **Comparative** is the form of the adjective or adverb used to say that someone or something is *bigger/quicker/more intelligent,* etc than someone or something else.
> **Superlative** is the form of the adjective or the adverb used for saying that someone or something is *best, quickest, biggest, most intelligent,* etc.

AGREEMENT (LES ACCORDS)

This is the word used for the way in which adjectives change their spelling to agree with (match) the noun they are describing, or the way a verb changes to agree with its subject. Past participles may also show agreement in the perfect and other compound tenses and in the passive form of the verb.

ARTICLES (LES ARTICLES)

There are three kinds of articles:
  Definite (L'article défini): *the*
  Indefinite (L'article indéfini): *a, an, some*
  Partitive (L'article partitif): *some, any*

CLAUSE (LA PROPOSITION)

These are parts of a sentence which contain a subject and a verb which agrees with that subject. In the sentence: "I said *that he should do it.*" the italicised phrase is the clause.

Grammatical Terms   *French Grammar*

CONJUNCTIONS (LES CONJONCTIONS)

These are words used to join sentences and clauses: *and, but, because, or, when.*

GENDER (LE GENRE)

There are two genders in French: masculine **le** and feminine **la**. All nouns are either masculine or feminine.

NOUNS (LES NOMS)

These are names of people, places and things.
They can be either **common (commun):** *boy, girl, bike, house*
or **proper (propre):** *Paris, François*
and either **abstract (abstrait):** *kindness, anger, justice,*
or **concrete (concrète):** *table, cow, car*

NUMBER (NOMBRE)

Things can be: **singular (singulier):** *one only*
plural (pluriel): *two or more*

PREPOSITIONS (LES PREPOSITIONS)

These are words placed in front of nouns and pronouns to show position and other relationships:

     in the garden   ***between*** the houses   ***on*** the floor
     before midnight   ***after*** 8 o'clock   ***around*** teatime

PRONOUNS (LES PRONOMS)

Pronouns fall into one of the following categories:

1. **Demonstrative (Des pronoms démonstratifs)**
   These pronouns are used to differentiate between: *this/that, these/those*

2. **Direct Object (Des pronoms de complément direct)**
   These show who or what is the recipient of the verb action:
   me, you, him, her, it, us, them
   Example: *I see **you***

3. **Emphatic (Les formes accentuées des pronoms)**
   These are a strong form of the pronoun used after a preposition or for emphasis where, in English, we would show emphasis with the voice.
   Example: *with **me***   *for **you***   *without **him***
   ***You** can't see him*

4. **Indirect Object (Des pronoms de complément indirect)**
   These are: *to me, to you, to him/her/it, to us, to them*
   Example: *I give it **to you***

5. **Indefinite (Des pronoms indéfinis)**
   These can be either the subject or the object of the verb.
   Example: *each one, someone, everything*

6. **Interrogative (Des pronoms interrogatifs)**
   These pronouns ask questions:
   Example: *Who?*

7. **Personal (Des pronoms personnels)**
   This is the general name given to subject, direct object, indirect object, reflexive pronouns:
   They can be   first person   *I, me, we, us*
                  second person   *you*
                  third person   *he, him, she, her, they, them*

8. **Possessive (Des pronoms possessifs)**
   These pronouns signify ownership:
   mine, yours, his, hers, ours, theirs

9. **Reflexive (Des pronoms refléchis)**
   These object pronouns refer back to the subject of the verb:
   myself, yourself, himself, herself, ourselves, yourselves, themselves

10. **Relative (Des pronoms relatifs)**
    These pronouns introduce a clause giving more information about a noun:
    who, which

11. **Subject (Des pronoms personnels - sujet)**
    These pronouns show who is performing the action of the verb:
    I, you, he, she, it, one, we, you, they

VERBS (LES VERBES)

Some students think that French verbs are difficult, but **if** you are prepared to give time to learning them thoroughly, you will find that even the irregular verbs follow certain patterns and that they are a valuable tool when speaking and writing the language.
A verb will tell you the actions and events in a sentence.
   Example: **Je joue** au football - ***I am playing** football*
               Il est arrivé à la maison - ***He arrived** at the house*
               Nous regardions la télévision - ***We were watching** TV*

There are some "technical" words which are used when talking about verbs:

Grammatical Terms *French Grammar*

Infinitive (L'infinitif)

This is the "name" of the verb and it is the form which is listed in a dictionary or verb table. It means "to ..."
  Example: **regarder** - *to look at, to watch*
The final two letters of the infinitive are important. They will tell you which conjugation or "family" the verb belongs to.

Conjugation (La conjugaison)

This is the term used to describe the different forms, tenses, moods and persons of the verb. It is the name given to the pattern which verbs follow.
There are three main conjugations in French: **-er, -ir,** and **-re**.
  Example: travaill**er**, fin**ir**, répond**re**
Many verbs belong to one or other of these groups, but many others are irregular.

Irregular verbs (Les verbes irreguliers)

These verbs, which do not follow one of the three patterns (**-er, -ir** and **-re**), are set out for you in the Verb Table at the back of the book. They are verbs which are frequently used and which you **must** know.
  Example: **venir** - *to come,* **voir** - *to see,* **rire** - *to laugh*

Object (Le complément)

This is the person or thing affected by the action of the verb.
The object of the sentence can be either a noun or a pronoun:
  Example: Nous mangeons **les pommes** *They eat **the apples***
       Nous **les** mangeons   *We eat **them***

Reflexive verbs (Les verbes pronominaux)

These are verbs which have an extra pronoun:
  Example: Je **me** lave; elle **s'**habille
These verbs are used to convey several types of ideas:

a) a truly reflexive action in which the subject performs the action to/for himself/herself, etc:
  Example: Nous **nous** lavons *We wash **ourselves***

b) a reciprocal action in which the subjects perform the action to/for each other:
  Example: Ils **se** regardent *They look at **each other***

c) avoidance of the passive:
  Example: Les crêpes **se mangent** en Bretagne *Crêpes **are eaten** in Brittany*

d) an action considered reflexive in French, although not necessarily so in English:
  Example: L'autobus **s'**arrête *The bus stops*

Subject (Le sujet)

This is the person or thing performing the action of the verb.
The subject can be either a noun or a pronoun:
>Example: **Les enfants** trouvent le chien. **Ils** le chassent
>*The children find the dog. They chase it*

Tenses (Les temps)

Tenses are the methods by which verbs tell you **when** events take place, will take place, took place, used to take place, etc. The names of the tenses are a guide to their use:
the **Present (le présent)** tells you what *is happening now*, or what *usually happens*
the **Future (le futur)** tells you what *will happen*
the **Perfect (le passé composé)** and the **Imperfect (l'imparfait)** tell you what *has happened* or *was happening* in the past.

Past participles (Les participes passés)

These are parts of a verb used with an **auxiliary verb (verbe auxiliaire)**, *avoir* or *être* to form the **Perfect (passé composé)** and **Pluperfect (plus-que-parfait)** tenses.
In English they often end in **-en, -ed** or **-t**   *given, looked, bought*
In French they often end in **-é, -i, -u, -s** or **-t**:
>donné   fini,   répondu,   pris   conduit

There are times when they agree (change their spelling).
Most irregular verbs have irregular past participles which have to be learned carefully.

>Example: voir becomes J'ai **vu**   écrire becomes J'ai **écrit**

Present participle (Le participe présent)

This is a part of the verb which ends in **-ing** in English, and **-ant** in French and is often used with **en**.
>Example: En sort**ant** de la maison, il ...   *While going out of the house, he ...*

Imperatives or Commands (L'imperatif)
These are the form of the verb you use when you are telling somebody (including yourself) to do something:
>Example: Regarde-moi!   *Look at me!*
>   Regardons la TV!   *Let's watch TV!*
>   Regardez les oiseaux-là!   *Look at those birds!*

Active or Passive (La voix active ou passive)
Verbs can be either active or passive.
Active means that the subject performs the action on or for the object:
>Example: Elle a trouvé le chien dans le parc
>   *She found the dog in the park*

Passive means that the subject is the recipient of the action:
>Example: Le chien a été trouvé dans le parc
>   *The dog has been found in the park*

The passive is used much more often in English than in French.

ADJECTIVES (LES ADJECTIFS)

Adjectives are words which are put with a noun to give you more information about it:
Example: la maison   la **petite** maison
          le chien   le **petit** chien **brun**

WATCH YOUR AGREEMENTS! (ATTENTION AUX ACCORDS!)

Adjectives in French alter their spelling to **agree with** (match) their noun.

Adjectives have different methods of showing agreement.

1. The most common way is to add **-e** to make the adjective feminine and **-s** to make it plural:

Masculine Singular	Feminine Singular	Masculine Plural	Feminine Plural	Meaning
Example: peti**t**	petite	petits	petites	*little*

   With adjectives which end in a consonant you have changes both in spelling and sound.

2. If the adjective already ends in **-u, -i** or **-é** the same spelling changes happen but there are no changes in the sound:

ms	fs	mpl	fpl	Meaning
Example: bleu	bleue	bleus	bleues	*blue*
joli	jolie	jolis	jolies	*pretty*
fermé	fermée	fermés	fermées	*closed*

3. If the adjective ends in **-e** there is no difference between the masculine and feminine singular, but an **-s** is added in the plural:

ms	fs	mpl	fpl	Meaning
Example: rouge	rouge	rouges	rouges	*red*

4. If the adjective ends in **-s**, there is no difference between the masculine singular and plural forms:

ms	fs	mpl	fpl	Meaning
Example: gris	grise	gris	grises	*grey*
anglais	anglaise	anglais	anglaises	*English*

5. Adjectives ending in **-eux** change to **-euse** in the feminine:

ms	fs	mpl	fpl	Meaning
Example: heureux	heureuse	heureux	heureuses	*happy*

6. Adjectives which end in **-er** or **-ier** change to **-ère** and **-ière** in the feminine:

ms	fs	mpl	fpl	Meaning
Example: cher	chère	chers	chères	*dear*
premier	première	premiers	premières	*first*

French Grammar *Adjectives*

7. Some adjectives double the consonant before adding -e:

	ms	fs	mpl	fpl	Meaning
Example:	ancien	ancienne	anciens	anciennes	*old, former*
	gentil	gentille	gentils	gentilles	*nice, kind*

8. Adjectives which end in **-f** or **-x** change their final letter before adding **-e** for the feminine:

	ms	fs	mpl	fpl	Meaning
Example:	sportif	sportive	sportifs	sportives	*athletic*
	jaloux	jalouse	jaloux	jalouses	*jealous*

9. Five common adjectives: **beau, nouveau, vieux, fou** and **mou** have an extra form of the **masculine singular** ‡ which you must use when the noun begins with a vowel or with a silent (mute) **h**. This is for ease of pronunciation. The plural is normal.

- beau, **bel** ‡, belle, beaux, belles

Example:	ms	le **beau** jardin	*the lovely garden*
	ms ‡	le **bel** arbre	*the lovely tree*
	fs	la **belle** maison	*the lovely house*
	mpl	les **beaux** jardins	*the lovely gardens*
	mpl	les **beaux** arbres	*the lovely trees*
	fpl	les **belles** maisons	*the lovely houses*

- nouveau, **nouvel** ‡, nouvelle, nouveaux, nouvelles

Example:	le **nouveau** vélo	*the new bike*
	le **nouvel** ‡ an	*the new year*

- vieux, **vieil** ‡, vieille, vieux, vieilles

Example:	le **vieux** monsieur	*the old gentleman*
	le **vieil** ‡ homme	*the old man*

- fou, **fol** ‡, folle, fous, folles

Example:	un prix **fou**	*an exorbitant (mad) price*
	un **fol** ‡ espoir	*a vain (mad) hope*

- mou, **mol** ‡, molle, mous, molles

Example:	le fromage **mou**	*soft cheese*
	un **mol** ‡ oreiller	*a soft pillow*

10. Unfortunately, some of the adjectives you will need to use frequently are irregular and you will have to learn them individually.

ms	fs	mpl	fpl	Meaning
blanc	blanche	blancs	blanches	*white*
complet	complète	complets	complètes	*complete*
doux	douce	doux	douces	*gentle*
favori	favorite	favoris	favorites	*favourite*
faux	fausse	faux	fausses	*false*
frais	fraîche	frais	fraîches	*cool, fresh*
long	longue	longs	longues	*long*
public	publique	publics	publiques	*public*
roux	rousse	roux	rousses	*red, auburn*
sec	sèche	secs	sèches	*dry*
secret	secrète	secrets	secrètes	*secret*

11. There are some adjectives which are invariable in gender or number, or both (they do not change their spelling).

a) chic *(smart)* is invariable in gender but does add **-s** for the plural:
Example: un chapeau **chic**/des chapeaux **chics** *a smart hat/smart hats*
une robe **chic**/des robes **chics** *a smart dress/smart dresses*

b) Adjectives made from nouns (often the names of fruit or flowers) are invariable in both gender and number: marron, noisette, cerise, orange, paille, pêche
Example: un manteau **marron** *a brown coat*
des yeux **marron** *brown eyes*

c) Cardinal numbers do not change their spelling:
Example: il y a **trente** élèves dans ma classe *there are 30 pupils in my class*

d) There is no change of spelling with compound adjectives of colour:
Example: une jupe **bleu marine/bleu clair**
a navy blue/light blue skirt
un pullover **bleu marine/bleu clair**
a navy blue/light blue pullover
des chaussettes **vert foncé/jaune pâle**
dark green/pale yellow socks

e) Notice the difference between:
des cravates **bleu et jaune** *blue and yellow* (two-colour) *ties*
and des cravates **bleues et jaunes** *blue and yellow ties*
(some are blue, some are yellow)

f) **nu-, demi-, mi-** are invariable when they are placed before a noun.
Example: il va **nu**-pieds   une **demi**-heure   la **mi**-janvier
he goes barefoot   half an hour   mid-January

French Grammar *Adjectives*

12. Adjectives themselves may have additional words put with them to add to or alter their meaning:
    Example: **cher**   *expensive*
              moins cher   *less expensive*
              très cher   *very expensive*
              trop cher   *too expensive*
              pas cher   *not expensive*
              si cher   *so expensive*
              tellement cher   *so expensive*
              de plus en plus cher   *more and more expensive*
              de moins en moins cher   *less and less expensive*
              extrêmement cher   *extremely expensive*

13. Some adjectives add a prefix to change their meaning to the opposite of the original:
    Example: heureux   *happy*   **mal**heureux   *unhappy*
              possible   *possible*   **im**possible   *impossible*
              croyable   *credible*   **in**croyable   *incredible*

POSITION OF ADJECTIVES (OÙ METTRE L'ADJECTIF?)

1. Adjectives usually **follow** their noun in French:
    Example: Il porte une chemise **blanche** et une cravate **rouge**
              He is wearing a white shirt and a red tie
              C'est une voiture **française**
              It is a French car

2. However, a few of the most frequently used adjectives are often placed **before** the noun:
    beau, bon, gentil, grand, gros, haut, jeune, joli, long, mauvais, nouveau, petit, premier (and other ordinal numbers), vieux, vilain *(ugly)*
    Example: C'est une **grande** maison   *a big house*
              une **jolie petite** fille   *a pretty little girl*

3. When you have a noun described by two adjectives, they will both take up their normal position:
    Example: une **jolie petite** maison   *a pretty little house*
              un **petit** animal **brun**   *a small brown animal*

4. If you are using two adjectives which follow the noun they should be linked by the word **et**. If there are more than two adjectives, only the final two are linked by **et**.
    Example: des élèves **intelligents et travailleurs**
              intelligent, hard-working pupils
              des élèves **intelligents, animés et travailleurs**
              intelligent, bright, hard-working pupils

9

Adjectives — French Grammar

5. There are some adjectives whose meaning changes according to whether they are put <u>before</u> or <u>after</u> the noun.
   These include:

   ancien, certain, cher, dernier, grand, nouveau, pauvre and **propre**

   Example: C'est mon **ancien** professeur   *He's my **ex**-teacher*
             C'est un bâtiment **ancien**   *It's an **old** building*

             un **certain** monsieur   *a **certain** gentleman*
             un fait **certain**   *a **definite** fact*

             un **cher** ami   *a **dear** friend*
             un pullover **cher**   *an **expensive** pullover*

             le **dernier** film de Spielberg   *Spielberg's **latest** film*
             le **dernier** jour de l'année   *the **last** day of the year*
             l'année **dernière**   ***last** year*

             un homme **grand**   *a **tall** man*
             un **grand** homme   *a **great** man*

             Le **Nouvel** An   *the **New** Year*
             Le Beaujolais **nouveau**   ***new** Beaujolais (this year's)*
             les pommes de terre **nouvelles**   ***new** potatoes*

             Le **pauvre** garçon est fatigué!   *The **poor** boy is tired!*
             Un garçon **pauvre**   *A **poor** boy (no money)*

             Il a sa **propre** chambre   *He has his **own** room*
             La chambre n'est pas **propre**   *The room is not **clean***

French Grammar *Adjectives*

COMPARISON OF ADJECTIVES (LA COMPARAISON DES ADJECTIFS)

Comparative adjectives (Adjectifs de comparaison)

To say that something is bigger, smaller, more expensive, etc, you put **plus** in front of the adjective. The adjective still takes its normal position in the sentence:

> Example: J'ai une **plus grande** voiture, mais il a une voiture **plus rapide**
> *I have a bigger car but he has a faster car*

To compare one thing with another you use:

> **plus ... que**   *more ... than*
> **moins ... que**   *less ... than*
> **aussi ... que**   *as ... as*

You must be careful to make the adjective agree as normal:

> Example: Mon frère est **plus** grand **que** ma sœur
> *My brother is bigger than my sister*
> Ma sœur est **moins** forte **que** mon frère
> *My sister is not as strong as my brother*
> Ma mère est **aussi** intelligente **que** mon père
> *My mother is as intelligent as my father*

You must use **si** in negative comparisons:

> Example: Elle **n'est pas si** grande que moi
> *She is **not as big as** I am*

There are some irregular comparatives:

- **bon** *good* becomes **meilleur** *better*

  > Example: Mick a une **bonne** idée, mais Val a une **meilleure** idée

- **mauvais** *bad* becomes either **pire** or **plus mauvais** *(worse)*
  Plus mauvais is used for *worse* in the sense of taste or quality:

  > Example: Cette histoire est **mauvaise**, mais l'autre est **pire**
  > Ce gâteau est **plus mauvais** que celui-là

- **petit** *small* also has two comparative forms: **plus petit** and **moindre**
  Plus petit is the one used for size.
  Moindre gives the idea of less in value/importance.

  > Example: Elle est **plus petite** que moi
  > *She is smaller than I am*
  > à **moindre** prix
  > *at a lower price*

Superlative adjectives (Les adjectifs de superlatif)

If you want to talk about *the best, the biggest, the least*, etc, you should use:
le plus/le moins ...
la plus/la moins ...
les plus/les moins ... followed by the adjective:

Example: le monument **le plus** célèbre de Londres
the most famous monument in London
la région **la plus** touristique
the region which is most popular with the tourists
les nouvelles **les moins** agréables
the worst news
La langue **la moins** difficile est ...
... is the least difficult language

Be careful with **bon, mauvais** and **petit**:
bon *(good)* becomes **le/la meilleur(e)**
mauvais *(bad)* becomes either **le plus mauvais** or **le pire**
petit *(small)* becomes either **le/la plus petit(e)** or **le/la moindre**

Example: le **meilleur** élève
the best pupil
la **meilleure** idée
the best idea

Le pire, c'est que ...
The worst of it is ...
C'est lui qui a **la plus mauvaise** chambre
He has the worst room
De nos deux voitures, la sienne est **la pire**
Of our two cars, his is the worst
De nos deux gâteaux, le mien est **le plus mauvais**
Mine is the worse of the two cakes

les plus petits enfants
the smallest children
Cela n'a pas **la moindre** importance
That hasn't the slightest importance

French Grammar *Adjectives*

MORE ADJECTIVES (ENCORE DES ADJECTIFS)

There are several other types of adjectives you may have to use.
They are: possessive adjectives, demonstrative adjectives, interrogative adjectives and adjectives which are used in exclamations.
Their names tell you the role they play in the sentence.

POSSESSIVE ADJECTIVES (LES ADJECTIFS POSSESSIFS)

These are the words you use with nouns to show ownership of an object. In English they are *my, your, his, her, its, our, their*. In French they each have three forms:

    Example: **mon** chien *my dog*, **ma** jupe *my skirt*, **mes** amis *my friends*

You choose the form according to the <u>gender of the thing owned</u> and not whether the owner is male or female! We <u>all</u> talk about **mon** père, **ma** mère, **mes** enfants, etc.

The full list of possessive adjectives reads:

	masc sing one object owned	fem sing	mpl/fpl several objects owned	Meaning	
one owner	mon	ma	mes	*my*	**one owner**
	ton	ta	tes	*your*	
	votre	votre	vos	*your (polite)*	
	son	sa	ses	*his, its*	
	son	sa	ses	*her, its*	
2+ owners	notre	notre	nos	*our*	**2+ owners**
	votre	votre	vos	*your*	
	leur	leur	leurs	*their*	

Remember:

1   When you have a **feminine** word beginning with a vowel or a silent **h**, you should use the **mon, ton, son** form of the possessive:
    Example: **mon** amie Louise   *my friend Louise*
                 ton idée   *your idea*
                 son intention   *his/her intention*

2   When you are talking about parts of the body you normally use the article rather than the possessive adjective:
    Example: Elle ouvre **les** yeux   *She opens her eyes*
                 J'ai tourné **la** tête   *I turned my head*
but in sentences where the part of the body is the subject of the verb you use the possessive:
    Example: **Ma** tête me fait mal   *My head hurts*
and if the part of the body has one or more adjectives describing it, you use the possessive:
    Example: **ses** (beaux) yeux bruns   *his/her (lovely) brown eyes*

Adjectives French Grammar

DEMONSTRATIVE ADJECTIVES (LES ADJECTIFS DÉMONSTRATIFS)

These are the words you use to demonstrate or show which object you are describing.
In English they are: *this, that, these, those*
In French they are:

masc sing	fem sing	masc pl	fem pl
ce, cet	cette	ces	ces

Since they are adjectives you must make them agree with their noun:
    Example: **ce** garçon, **cet** arbre, **cet** hôtel
                      cette maison
                      ces arbres, **ces** garçons, **ces** maisons

1. The extra masculine singular form is used when the masculine noun begins with a vowel or a silent **h:**
    Example: **cet** arbre, **cet** enfant, **cet** homme, **cet** hôtel
but in the plural you use the normal form of the adjective:
                      ces arbres, **ces** enfants, **ces** hommes, **ces** hôtels

2. To put real emphasis on **this** as opposed to **that** you add **-ci** or **-là** to the noun:
    Example: **ce** livre-**ci**   *this book*
                      cette robe-**là**   *that dress*

3. You must also remember to repeat the correct adjective with each noun in a list:
    Example: Où as-tu trouvé **ce** livre et **ces** classeurs?
                      Where did you find this book and these folders?

INTERROGATIVE ADJECTIVES (LES ADJECTIFS INTERROGATIFS)

These are words which help you to ask questions about things.
In English we say *which?* or *what?*
In French the words are :

masc sing	fem sing	masc pl	fem pl
quel?	quelle?	quels?	quelles?

These words are adjectives and must agree with their nouns:
    Example: **Quel** chien as-tu vu?
                  Which dog did you see?
                  Quelle est la date de ton anniversaire?
                  What is the date of your birthday?
                  Quels sont les animaux que tu aimes le mieux?
                  Which animals do you like best?
                  Quelles maisons?
                  Which houses?

It is worth noticing that these words are used in exclamations as well as in questions:
    Example: **Quel** dommage!   *What a pity!*
                  Quelle idée!   *The very idea!*
                  Quels beaux animaux!   *What beautiful animals!*
                  Quelles belles fleurs!   *What beautiful flowers!*

French Grammar   *Adjectives*

INDEFINITE ADJECTIVES (LES ADJECTIFS INDÉFINIS)

Here are some of the most common indefinite adjectives with phrases to show you how they are used:

Chaque   (invariable)
Example: **chaque** jour
each day
chaque maison
each house

Quelque, quelques
Example: **quelque** part
somewhere
à **quelque** distance de la maison
some distance from the house
à **quelques** kilomètres de la ville
some kilometres from the town

Tel, telle, tels, telles
The word order is **un tel, une telle** where we might say *such a ...* or *like that*.
Example: Avec un **tel** vélo, on pourrait gagner des courses
You could win races with a bike like that
Avec une **telle** voiture, on roule très vite
You go fast in a car like that

Note that **des** changes to **de** in the plural here because **tels/telles** comes before the noun.
Example: De **tels** animaux sont dangereux
Such animals are dangerous
de **telles** femmes
such women

Use **tel** if that is the only adjective but **si** if there are two or more adjectives.
Example: une **telle** maison
such a house/a house like that
une **si belle petite** fille
such a beautiful little girl

Tout, toute, tous, toutes
Example: **tout** le gâteau   *all the/the whole cake*
toute la journée   *all day/the whole day*
tous les animaux   *all the animals*
tous les jours   *every day*
toutes les filles   *all the girls*

ADVERBS (LES ADVERBES)

Adverbs are words added to verbs, adjectives and other adverbs to tell you more about how, when, where a thing is/was done.
Adverbs in English usually end in -**ly**.
In French they usually end in -**ment**.

Example: Il parle **poliment** *He speaks **politely***
Elle marche **lentement** *She walks **slowly***

FORMATION OF ADVERBS (LA FORMATION DES ADVERBES)

1. Adverbs are often formed by using the feminine form of the adjective as a basis and adding -**ment**:

Masc adj	**Fem adj**	**Adverb**	**Meaning**
Example: heureux	heureuse	heureusement	*fortunately*
malheureux	malheureuse	malheureusement	*unfortunately*
doux	douce	doucement	*gently*

2. Some adjectives change their final -**e** to -**é** before adding –**ment**:

Adjective	**Adverb**	**Meaning**
Example: précise	précisément	*precisely*
profonde	profondément	*deeply*
énorme	énormément	*enormously*

3. If the adjective ends in a vowel, the adverb is formed by adding -**ment** to the masculine form:

Adjective	**Adverb**	**Meaning**
Example: poli	poliment	*politely*
vrai	vraiment	*truly, really*

4. If the masculine form of the adjective ends in -**ant**, the adverb ends in -**amment**:

Adjective	**Adverb**	**Meaning**
Example: constant	constamment	*constantly*

5. If the masculine form of the adjective ends in -**ent**, the adverb ends in -**emment** (pronounced -**a**mment):

Adjective	**Adverb**	**Meaning**
Example: prudent	prudemment	*wisely, prudently*
évident	évidemment	*obviously, evidently*

6. There are adverbs which do not follow the rules and you must learn these carefully because they are often used.

Adverb	**Meaning**	**Adverb**	**Meaning**
Example: avec soin	*carefully*	mieux	*better*
beaucoup	*much, a lot*	souvent	*often*
bien	*well*	toujours	*still, always*
longtemps	*for a long time*	trop	*too much*
mal	*badly*	vite	*quickly*

French Grammar   *Adverbs*

POSITION OF ADVERBS (OÙ METTRE LES ADVERBES?)

It is not easy to make a hard and fast rule about where to put the adverb in a sentence because so much depends on the emphasis you wish to make.
However there are guidelines which will help you:

1. In a sentence with the verb in a simple tense, the adverb is generally put **after** the verb it is to emphasise:

    Example: Il va **souvent** à la piscine
    He often goes to the swimming pool
    Il va nager **souvent**
    He goes swimming often
    Elle se tenait **longtemps** devant le cinéma
    She was standing outside the cinema for a long time
    A quatre heures nous sortons **vite** du collège
    We come out of school quickly at four o'clock

2. In sentences where the verb is in a compound tense (the perfect and pluperfect tenses), long adverbs, adverbs of place and common adverbs of time such as **tard** *late*, **hier** *yesterday*, **aujourd'hui** *today*, all **follow** the past participle:

    Example: Elle a parlé **doucement** à l'animal
    She spoke gently to the animal
    Nous l'avons cherché **partout**
    We looked everywhere for him
    Je suis arrivé **tard**
    I arrived late
    Il est parti **hier**
    He left yesterday
    Elle est arrivée **aujourd'hui**
    She arrived today

3. Fairly short, common adverbs such as **souvent** *often*, **vite** *quickly*, **beaucoup** *a lot*, **trop** *too much* and **tout à fait** *completely* come **before** the past participle:

    Example: Elle a **souvent** parlé
    She often talked
    Je l'avais **vite** oublié
    I had quickly/soon forgotten it
    Il a **beaucoup** parlé
    He talked a lot
    Elle a **trop** parlé
    She talked too much
    Je l'avais **tout à fait** oublié
    I had completely forgotten it

Adverbs   *French Grammar*

COMPARISON OF ADVERBS (LA COMPARAISON DES ADVERBES)

Comparative Adverbs (Les adverbes de comparaison)

The **Comparative** is formed by using **plus ... que, moins ... que,** or **aussi ... que** with the adverb:

>Example: Mon frère nage **plus** vite **que** ma mère
>*My brother swims **more** quickly **than** my mother*
>Je cours **moins** vite **que** mon fils
>*I run **less** quickly **than** my son*
>Mon mari conduit **aussi** bien **que** son frère
>*My husband drives **as** well **as** his brother*

Superlative Adverbs (Les adverbes de superlatif)

The **Superlative** is formed by using **le plus, le moins** with the adverb:

>Example: Il court **le plus vite**
>*He runs **the fastest***
>Je vais **le moins souvent** à la piscine
>*I go to the swimming pool **least often***

There are some irregular comparisons which you should learn:

Beaucoup *a lot* becomes **plus** *more* and **le plus** *most*

>Example: Je parle **beaucoup**
>*I talk a lot*
>Ma sœur parle **plus**
>*My sister talks **more***
>C'est mon frère qui parle **le plus**
>*It is my brother who talks **most***

Bien *well* becomes **mieux** *better* and **le mieux** *best*

>Example: L'équipe anglaise a joué **bien**
>*The English team played well*
>L'équipe indienne a joué **mieux**
>*The Indian team played better*
>L'équipe australienne a joué **le mieux**
>*The Australian team played best*

French Grammar *Adverbs*

MORE ADVERBS (ENCORE DES ADVERBES)

alors	Il habitait à Paris **alors**	*He lived in Paris then*
assez	Il est **assez** grand Il travaille **assez** dur	*He is quite big* *He works quite hard*
bien	**bien** sûr J'ai **bien** reçu votre lettre	*of course* *I have received your letter*
beaucoup	Il mange **beaucoup** **beaucoup de** cadeaux **beaucoup d'**enfants	*He eats a lot* *many presents/a lot of presents* *many children/a lot of children*
combien	**Combien** de pommes as-tu mangé? **Combien** de fois?	*How many apples did you eat?* *How many times?*
comme	**Comme** il fait froid!	*How cold it is!*
comment	**Comment** ça va? **Comment** t'appelles-tu? **Comment!** Qu'est-ce que tu as dit?	*How are you?* *What is your name?* *What! What did you say?*
encore	C'est **encore** plus difficile Le train n'est pas **encore** arrivé **encore** une fois	*It's even more difficult* *The train has not yet arrived* *once more*
en retard	J'arrive toujours **en retard**!	*I'm always late!*
où	la ville **où** j'habite D'**où** viens-tu?	*the town where I live* *Where do you come from?*
peu	J'ai **peu** d'argent Elle mange **peu**	*I haven't got much money* *She doesn't eat much*
plutôt	Le jardin est **plutôt** petit	*The garden is rather small*
quand	**Quand** arrive-t-il? C'est pour **quand**?	*When is he coming?* *When is it for?*
tant	Il a besoin de **tant** d'argent	*He needs so much money*
tard	Lui, il se couche **tard**	*He goes to bed late*
tôt	Je me lève **tôt** le matin	*I get up early in the morning*
toujours	Je sors **toujours** le samedi soir Il est **toujours** à la maison	*I always go out on Saturday evening* *He is still at home*

ARTICLES (LES ARTICLES)

There are three types of article you will need to be able to use.

THE DEFINITE ARTICLE (L'ARTICLE DÉFINI)

This is the equivalent of the English *the*.

Le is used with masculine nouns which begin with a consonant:
>**le** garçon, **le** mur, **le** chien

La is used with feminine nouns which begin with a consonant:
>**la** fille, **la** maison, **la** robe

L' is used with both masculine and feminine nouns which begin with a vowel or a silent (mute) **h**:
>**l'**homme (m), **l'**arbre (m), **l'**heure (f), **l'**église (f)

Les is always used with nouns in the plural whether masculine or feminine:
>**les** hommes (m) **les** garçons (m)
>**les** filles (f) **les** maisons (f)

The definite article is needed:

1. with nouns which refer to a particular object or person:
   Example: **Le** garçon est dans **le** jardin
   The boy is in the garden

2. with nouns (both abstract and concrete) used in a general sense:
   Example: **L'**histoire m'intéresse mais je préfère **la** géographie
   I find history interesting, but I prefer geography
   J'aime **les** chats, mais ma fille préfère **les** chiens
   I like cats but my daughter prefers dogs

3. with countries and languages:
   Example: **L'**Angleterre est plus petite que **la** France
   England is smaller than France
   J'apprends **le** français depuis cinq ans
   I have been learning French for five years

4. when speaking about parts of the body:
   Example: Je me lave **le** visage
   I wash my face
   Elle a **les** yeux bruns et **les** cheveux noirs
   She has brown eyes and black hair

5. in phrases using people's names or titles:
   Example: **La** reine Elizabeth   *Queen Elizabeth*
   Le président de Gaulle   *President de Gaulle*
   Le pauvre Paul - il est malade   *Poor Paul - he is ill!*

French Grammar *Articles*

Le and les with à and des

When **le** and **les** are used with **à** to mean *to/at the*, there have to be spelling changes for **à+le** and **à+les**:
    Example: Je vais **au** magasin (=à+le)   *I go to the shop*
                  Je vais **aux** magasins (=à+les) *I go to the shops*
                  Il arrive **au** Havre (=à+le)   *He arrives at Le Havre*

No spelling changes are needed for **à+la or à+l'**:
    Example: Elle va **à la** porte   *She goes to the door*
                  Il parle **à l'**enfant   *He talks to the child*
                  Elle reste **à la** maison   *She is staying at home*

When **le** and **les** are used with **de** there have to be spelling changes for **de+le** and **de+les**:
    Example: en face **du** bureau (=de+le)   *opposite the office*
                  en haut **des** collines (=de+les) *at the top of the hills*
                  Il part **du** Havre (=de+le)   *He leaves from Le Havre*

No spelling changes are needed for **de+la** and **de+l'**
    Example: en face **de la** banque   *opposite the bank*
                  en face **de l'**église   *opposite the church*

THE INDEFINITE ARTICLE (L'ARTICLE INDÉFINI)

In the singular, **un/une** is the equivalent of the English *a, an, any*
In the plural, **des** is the equivalent of the English *some, any*
Un is used with masculine nouns, **une** with feminine nouns and **des** with all plural nouns.
    Example: J'ai **un** chien qui s'appelle Sam
                  I have a dog called Sam
                  Elle a **une** maison à la campagne
                  She has a house in the country
                  Nous avons acheté **des** pommes, **des** citrons et **des** bananes
                  We bought apples, lemons and bananas

Notice: In French, the article is needed before each noun in a list.

You will notice that there are times when the article is **not** needed in French where we would use it in English:

1.   When stating a person's job:
        Example: Il est professeur
                  He is a teacher

2.   Before numbers such as **cent** or **mille**:
        Example: Il y a mille élèves au collège
                  There are a thousand pupils in the school
                  J'ai cent euros
                  I have a hundred euros

Articles *French Grammar*

3. With words such as **sans** and **quelques**:
    Example: Il est arrivé sans voiture
    He arrived without a car
    Quelques minutes plus tard
    A few minutes later

4. In exclamations:
    Example: Quelle bonne idée! Quel dommage!
    What a good idea! What a shame!

Notice that **un/une/des** must all be replaced by **de/d'** if the verb in the sentence is negative:

Example:	J'ai **un** frère	changes to	Je n'ai pas **de** frère
	I have a brother		*I have no brother*
	J'ai **une** soeur	changes to	Je n'ai pas **de** soeur
	I have a sister		*I have no sister*
	J'ai **des** animaux	changes to	Je n'ai pas **d'**animaux
	I have animals		*I have no animals*

THE PARTITIVE ARTICLE (L'ARTICLE PARTITIF)

This is the equivalent of the English *some* or *any*
There are several forms of this article:

du is used for masculine nouns:
   Example: J'ai acheté **du** pain
   I have bought some bread

de la is used for feminine nouns:
   Example: Elle mange **de la** viande
   She is eating (some) meat

de l' is used for both masculine and feminine singular nouns which begin with a vowel:
   Example: As-tu **de l'**argent?
   Have you got any money?
   Elle cherche **de l'**eau
   She is looking for water

des is used for both masculine and feminine nouns in the plural:
   Example: J'ai **des** frères; il a **des** soeurs
   I have brothers; he has sisters

There are occasions when you must use **de** or **d'** instead of these forms:

When your verb is negative:
Example: Je n'ai pas **de** pain
I haven't got any bread
Elle ne mange pas **de** viande
She doesn't eat any meat
Elle ne cherche pas **d'**eau
She isn't looking for (any) water
Je n'ai pas **de** frères; il n'a pas **de** soeurs
I haven't got any brothers; he hasn't got any sisters

When, in the plural, the adjective you are using comes before the noun, you must use **de** instead of **des**:
Example: J'ai vu **de** grands magasins près de l'hôtel
I saw some big shops near the hotel
Ce sont **de** bons amis
They are good friends

When you are talking about specific quantities you use **de** or **d'**:
Example: Un kilo **de** tomates
a kilo of tomatoes
500 grammes **de** jambon
500 grams of ham
Beaucoup **de** poires
a lot of pears
beaucoup **d'**oranges
a lot of oranges

Other words which use **de/d'** in this way include:-
combien de? trop de... un peu de... assez de...

Example: Il y a **combien d'**enfants?
How many children are there?
Il y a **trop d'**animaux
There are too many animals
Il a **un peu d'**argent
He has a little money
As-tu **assez de** monnaie?
Have you enough change?

CONJUNCTIONS (LES CONJONCTIONS)

The most common conjunctions (joining words) in French are:

alors que	On m'a téléphoné **alors que** je travaillais dans le jardin The phone rang ***just as/while*** *I was working in the garden*
car	Il est content **car** il ne peut pas aller à l'école *He is happy **because** he can't go to school*
comme	Je l'ai vu **comme** je sortais de la maison *I saw him **as** I was leaving the house*
dès que	**Dès que** je la regarde, elle se met en colère ***As soon as** I look at her, she gets angry*
donc	J'ai mal à la tête, **donc** je reste à la maison ce soir *I have a headache **so** I'm staying at home this evening*
et	J'ai des crayons, un stylo **et** une gomme *I have pencils, a pen **and** a rubber* (no comma before **et**)
lorsque	**Lorsqu'**il est entré ... **Lorsqu'**il entrera ... ***When** he came in ... **When** he comes in ...*
mais	Il est grand, **mais** elle est petite *He is big, **but** she is small*
or	**Or,** ce garçon avait un chien énorme ... ***Now,** this boy had an <u>enormous</u> dog ...*
ou	Je vous écrirai **ou** je vous téléphonerai la semaine prochaine *I'll write to you **or** I'll ring you next week*
parce que	Il est content, **parce qu'**il va partir en vacances *He is happy **because** he is going on holiday*
pendant que	**Pendant que** je préparais le repas ... ***While** I was getting the meal ready ...*
puisque	**Puisqu'**il est venu, il faut lui parler *As he has come, we must speak to him*
quand	**Quand** j'y arriverai, je lui parlerai ***When** I get there, I will speak to her/to him* (See page 68)
tandis que	Lui, il adore le jazz, **tandis que** moi, je préfère la musique classique <u>He</u> *likes jazz **while** I prefer classical music*

NOUNS (LES NOMS)

Nouns in French are either:

Masculine (le, l', un)			or	Feminine (la, l', une)		
le garçon	un garçon	*boy*		la fille	une fille	*girl*
le chien	un chien	*dog*		la poule	une poule	*hen*
le crayon	un crayon	*pencil*		la chaise	une chaise	*chair*
l'arbre	un arbre	*tree*		l'église	une église	*church*

In word lists words are usually given their definite article: **le** or **la**:
    Example: **le jardin, la maison**
However, if the noun begins with a vowel the noun is sometimes shown with the indefinite article **un** or **une** because **l'** does not make the gender clear.
Alternatively the gender may be shown in brackets after the noun.
    Example: **un arbre, une église** or **l'arbre (m), l'église (f)**

GENDER PROBLEMS (LES PROBLÈMES DE GENRE)

The learning of genders is not easy for speakers of English. There are rules which can help you with this task, but the only sure way of getting it right is to learn the gender of each noun when you meet the word for the first time.

    Learn: **le** garçon, **la** voiture, **un** arbre, **une** église, etc

There are some general guidelines which can make life easier!

1. Names of males are usually masculine and names of females are usually feminine:
le père, **le** frère, **la** mère, **la** sœur,
except in some jobs such as Madame **le** Ministre, Madame **le** Maire

2. However, sometimes the same word may have either **le** or **la** depending on whether it refers to a man or a woman:
| un élève | *pupil (boy)* | une élève | *pupil (girl)* |
| le propriétaire | *owner (man)* | la propriétaire | *owner (woman)* |

whereas other words do not change their gender.
They are always **le** or **la** no matter whether the person is man or woman:
un auteur	*author, writer*	*man or woman*
le chef	*leader, boss, chief, chef*	*man or woman*
le médecin	*the doctor*	*man or woman*
la personne	*the person*	*man or woman*
le professeur	*the teacher*	*man or woman*

(but, in less formal speech, you will hear **le** prof or **la** prof)

3. Nouns for animals generally have one gender whatever their sex:
    Example: **un** animal, **un** éléphant, **une** girafe, **une** souris, etc.
and you just have to learn which is which.

Nouns   French Grammar

4. Some familiar domestic and wild animals do have a modified form for each sex:
   Example: **le** lion/**la** lionne   **le** chien/**la** chienne   **le** chat/**la** chatte

   Notice that **le coq** *cockerel*, **la poule** *hen*, **le taureau** *bull*, **la vache** *cow* have different words for the two sexes and not just different spellings of the same word.

5. **Masculine nouns include:**

   - Names of countries and rivers **not** ending in -e
     le Japon, le Canada, le Rhin
     (exceptions: le Cambodge, le Mexique, le Zaïre)
   - The days of the week
   - The months of the year
   - The seasons
   - Fractions
   - Measurements and weights in the metric system
     (exception: **la** tonne)
   - Metals
   - Points of the compass
   - Trees, flowers, fruits not ending in -e

6. **Some Masculine word endings**

   Nouns ending in the following ways are usually masculine:

-acle	le spectacle
-age	le fromage, le nuage, le village
	(exceptions: la cage, la page, la plage, la rage, une image)
-ail	le travail
-ain	le copain
-eau	le tableau, le rideau, le gâteau, le château
	(exceptions: l'eau, la peau)
-ège	le collège
-eil	le soleil, un appareil
-ème	le problème
-ent	l'agent, le serpent
-et	le jouet, le guichet
-eur	(concrete nouns) le facteur, un ordinateur
-ien	un Italien, un chien
-ier	l'atelier, le papier
-isme	le tourisme, le cyclisme
-ment	l'appartement, le bâtiment
-oir	le couloir, le tiroir
-our	l'amour, le tour *trick, tour, turn*
	(exceptions: la cour, la tour *tower*)

French Grammar   *Nouns*

7. **Feminine nouns include:**

   - Names of countries and rivers ending in **-e**:
     la France, l'Italie, la Seine (exception: le Rhône)
   - Names of flowers, fruits and vegetables ending in **-e**:
     la jonquille, la fraise, la carotte

8. **Some Feminine word endings**

   Words ending in the following ways are usually feminine:

-aison	la maison, la saison
-ance	la chance, la distance, les vacances
-anse	la danse
-ée	la journée, l'entrée (exceptions: le lycée, le musée)
-ence	l'essence, la patience (exception: le silence)
-ette	la baguette, la chaussette
-eur	(abstract nouns) la peur, la longueur
-ie	la sortie (exception: un incendie *fire*)
-ille	la famille
-ise	la bêtise
-itude	l'habitude
-té	(abstract nouns) la bonté *kindness*
-tion	la natation
-trice	l'actrice
-sion	une excursion, la permission
-xion	la connexion

MASCULINE NOUNS AND THEIR FEMININE FORMS
(LES NOMS MASCULINS AVEC LEURS FORMES FÉMININES)

1. The usual way to make the feminine form of a masculine noun is to add **-e** to the masculine form, and of course change the article from le/un to la/une:
   Example: un ami   une amie
                 le cousin   la cousine

2. Masculine nouns ending in **-e** show no change in the feminine form:
   Example: un élève   une élève

3. Masculine nouns ending in **-p** or **-f** change the **-p** or **-f** to **-v** before adding the **-e**:
   Example: le loup *wolf*   la louve *she-wolf*
                 le veuf *widower*   la veuve *widow*

4. Masculine nouns ending in **-er** have the feminine form in **-ère**:
   Example: le boulanger   la boulangère   *baker*

5. Masculine nouns ending in **-eau** have the feminine form in **-elle**:
   Example: le jumeau   la jumelle   *twin*

6. Masculine nouns ending in **-oux** and **-eur** have **-ouse** and **-euse** as their feminine forms:
   Example: un époux *husband*   une épouse *wife*
             un danseur *dancer*   une danseuse *dancer*

7. Most masculine nouns ending in **-teur** have the feminine form in **-trice**:
   Example: un acteur *actor*   une actrice *actress*
             un directeur   une directrice
             Headmaster   *Headmistress*

8. Masculine nouns ending in **-ien** or **-ion** can double the **-n** before adding **-e**:
   Example: un Canadien   une Canadienne
             un lion *lion*   une lionne *lioness*

9. Some masculine nouns have completely irregular feminine forms:
   Example: le fils   *son*   la fille   *daughter*
             le héros   *hero*   l'héroïne   *heroine*
             (aspirate h)   (silent h)
             le mari   *husband*   la femme   *wife*
             le roi   *king*   la reine   *queen*

Additional information about genders

1. Some words have two genders and two meanings:
   Example: le livre   *book*   la livre   *£ Sterling*
             le manche   *handle*   la manche   *sleeve*
                                              la Manche   *the Channel*
             le pendule   *pendulum*   la pendule   *clock*
             le poste   *job*   la Poste   *post office*
             le tour   *trick, tour, turn* la tour   *tower*
             le voile   *veil*   la voile   *sail*
             le vase   *vase*   la vase   *mud*

2. Note that you say: **la** chose (f) *(thing)*
   but   quelque chose de **bon** *something good*

3. Festivals: Noël   *Christmas* is masculine
                Joyeux Noël   *Happy Christmas*
   but   à la Noël   *at Christmas* (short for à la fête de Noël)
                Pâques   *Easter* is masculine
   but   Joyeuses Pâques   *Happy Easter*

French Grammar *Nouns*

PLURAL OF NOUNS (LE PLURIEL DES NOMS)

When you are writing French, it is vital to notice whether nouns are masculine or feminine, singular or plural because their adjectives must agree and you must also choose the correct verb forms.

1. To make nouns plural you change the form of the article and that of the noun itself.

   The definite articles **le**, **la**, and **l'** all change to **les**:

   Example: **les** garçons, **les** arbres, **les** filles, **les** églises
   the boys, the trees, the girls, the churches

   The indefinite articles **un** and **une** become **des**:

   Example: **des** garçons, **des** arbres, **des** filles, **des** églises
   some boys, some trees, some girls, some churches

   or **de** if there is an adjective preceding the noun:

   Example: **de** bonnes idées   *some good ideas*
   de grands arbres   *some big trees*
   de jolies fleurs   *some pretty flowers*

2. The most usual way of making a noun plural is to add **-s** to the singular:
   Example: les arbres, les filles, les maisons

3. Nouns which end in **-s**, **-x**, **-z** show no change:
   Example: les bras *arms*, les voix *voices*, les nez *noses*

4. Nouns whose singular ends in **-eau** or **-eu** add **-x** to become plural:
   Example: les oiseaux *birds* les feux *fires*
   (exception: les pneus *tyres*)

5. Nouns with a singular which ends in **-ail** or **-iel** change as follows:
   Example: le travail   les travaux
   le ciel   les cieux

6. Nouns with a singular which ends in **-al** change as follows:

   l'animal (m)   les animaux
   le cheval   les chevaux
   le journal   les journaux
   l'hôpital (m)   les hôpitaux
   (exceptions include: les **bals**, les **carnavals**)

29

Nouns   *French Grammar*

7.   Nouns whose singular ends in **-ou** generally add **-s**
        Example: les cous *necks,* les trous *holes*
                 (exceptions include: les bijoux *jewels*
                                      les cailloux *pebbles*
                                      les choux *cabbages*
                                      les genoux *knees*)

COMPOUND NOUNS (LES NOMS COMPOSÉS)

This is the name given to nouns which are made up from various elements:
noun + noun, verb + noun, etc.
When you meet compound nouns, the best way is to learn each one with its plural because there are various patterns for forming compound nouns, and the plurals vary according to how the compound noun is made up.
It is only the part which is itself either a noun or an adjective which can change. The part which is a verb or preposition cannot change:

    Example: **le chou-fleur** *cauliflower* is a noun + a noun so both parts change:
                  les choux-fleurs
                  le tire-bouchon *corkscrew* is a verb + a noun so -s is added only to the
                  second word: **les tire-bouchons**
                  la machine à coudre *sewing machine* is a noun + à + a verb so only the
                  first element changes: **les machines à coudre**

It might be sensible to learn these common compound nouns together with their plurals:

                la garde-robe   les garde-robes   *wardrobe*
                le lave-vaisselle   les lave-vaisselle   *dishwasher*
                le timbre-poste   les timbres-poste   *stamp*
                la auberge de jeunesse   les auberges de jeunesse   *youth hostel*
                le chemin de fer   les chemins de fer   *railway*
                la pomme de terre   les pommes de terre   *potato*
                la chambre à coucher   les chambres à coucher   *bedroom*
                la planche à voile   les planches à voile   *sailboard*
                la tasse à café   les tasses à café   *coffee cup*

Irregularities (Quelques particularités)

1.   Notice these words which do not show any change in the plural:
        Example: Il est chez les **Beauchamp**
                       *He is staying with the **Beauchamps***
                       Le mot "jette" s'écrit avec 2 "**t**"
                       *"jette" is written with **2 t's***
                       Il a perdu cinq livres **sterling**
                       *He has lost **£5***

French Grammar *Nouns*

2. Some words are always plural in French:
   Example: les arrhes *deposit*
   les frais *expenses*
   les gens *people*
   les mathématiques *maths*

3. Some words change their meaning depending on whether they are singular or plural:
   Example: **le** devoir *duty*
   les devoirs *homework*
   (but: **le** devoir de français *French homework*)
   la vacance *vacancy*
   les vacances *holiday(s)*

4. Notice the plural of the following:

Monsieur	becomes	Messieurs
Madame	becomes	Mesdames
Mademoiselle	becomes	Mesdemoiselles

Collective nouns (Des noms collectifs)

Some nouns are singular in form although they are plural in meaning and they therefore take a singular verb in French.
Three common ones are : la famille, la police and la foule

   Example: La famille **est** à la maison   *The family is at home*
   La police **est** arrivée   *The police arrived*
   La foule **attendait**   *The crowd was waiting*

The Possessive Case

To show ownership there is no equivalent of the apostrophe **s** which we have in English. Instead, with proper names, you have to use the word **de**:

   Example: le chapeau **de** Jean   *Jean's hat*
   la jupe **d'**Anne   *Anne's skirt*

With other nouns you use **de** + the article.
This means that you have to be careful with masculine and plural nouns:

   Example: le chien **du** garçon   *the boy's dog*   (1 dog, 1 boy)
   le chien **de la** fille   *the girl's dog*   (1 dog, 1 girl)
   le chien **de l'**enfant   *the child's dog*   (1 dog, 1 child)
   le chien **des** enfants   *the children's dog* (1 dog, more than 1 child)
   le chien **des** garçons   *the boys' dog*   (1 dog, more than 1 boy)
   le chien **des** filles   *the girls' dog*   (1 dog, more than 1 girl)

NUMBERS, TIMES AND DATES
(LES NOMS DE NUMÉRO, L'HEURE ET LA DATE)

CARDINAL NUMBERS (LES NOMS DE NUMÉRO)

0	zéro	20	vingt	80	quatre-vingts
1	un, une	21	vingt et un	81	quatre-vingt-un
2	deux	22	vingt-deux	82	quatre-vingt-deux
3	trois	23	vingt-trois	90	quatre-vingt-dix
4	quatre	24	vingt-quatre	91	quatre-vingt-onze
5	cinq	25	vingt-cinq	92	quatre-vingt-douze
6	six	26	vingt-six	100	cent
7	sept	27	vingt-sept	101	cent un
8	huit	28	vingt-huit	105	cent cinq
9	neuf	29	vingt-neuf	150	cent cinquante
10	dix	30	trente	300	trois cents
11	onze	31	trente et un	308	trois cent huit
12	douze	40	quarante	1000	mille
13	treize	41	quarante et un	1203	mille deux cent trois
14	quatorze	50	cinquante	1990	mille neuf cent quatre-vingt-dix
15	quinze	60	soixante		
16	seize	70	soixante-dix	2004	deux mille quatre
17	dix-sept	71	soixante et onze	5000	cinq mille
18	dix-huit	72	soixante-douze	1,000,000	un million
19	dix-neuf	79	soixante-dix-neuf	1,000,000,000	un milliard

You should learn the following points:

1. vingt et un, trente et un, quarante et un, cinquante et un, soixante et un, soixante et onze are **not** hyphenated

2. quatre-vingt-un and quatre-vingt-onze **are** hyphenated

3. Fractions/les fractions:
   - 1/2 un demi (only in arithmetic)
   - In other contexts you should use **une moitié**
   - but **demi** is used as an adjective in the words
   - une **demi**-bouteille *(half a bottle, a half bottle)*
   - and une **demi**-heure *(half an hour, a half hour)*
   - 1/4 un quart
   - 1/3 un tiers (Le Tiers Monde - *the Third World*)
   - 2/3 deux tiers
   - 3/4 trois quarts

4. mille does not have a plural form

5. Telephone numbers are read out in groups of two or three:
   Example: 02.62.94.50.70
   would be read as:
   zéro deux/soixante-deux/quatre-vingt-quatorze/cinquante/soixante-dix

French Grammar *Numbers, Time and Dates*

ORDINAL NUMBERS (ADJECTIFS NUMÉRAUX)

In English, these are the words *first, second, third, fourth, sixth, etc.*
In French, these are formed usually by adding **-ième** to the cardinal number:
  Example: deuxième, troisième, etc

but with numbers ending in **-e,** the final **-e** of the cardinal number is removed :
  Example: quatrième, douzième

Notice also:
  1st has two forms: premier (masculine) and première (feminine)
  2nd has two forms: deuxième and seconde
  5th   cinquième
  9th   neuvième
  31st   trente et **unième**

Pupils in school would say:
  Je suis en sixième   *I am in Year 7*
  Je suis en seconde   *I am in Year 11*
  Je suis en première   *I am in Year 12 (Lower Sixth)*
  Je suis en terminale   *I am in Year 13 (Upper Sixth)*

TELLING THE TIME (L'HEURE)

  Quelle heure est-il?   *What time is it?*
  Il est une heure   *It is one o'clock*
  Il est deux heures   *It is two o'clock*
  Il est trois heures cinq   *It is 5 past 3*
  Il est cinq heures dix   *It is 10 past 5*
  Il est six heures et quart   *It is quarter past 6*
  Il est sept heures vingt   *It is 20 past 7*
  Il est huit heures vingt-cinq   *It is 25 past 8*
  Il est neuf heures et demie   *It is half past 9*
  Il est dix heures moins vingt-cinq   *It is 25 to 10*
  Il est onze heures moins vingt   *It is 20 to 11*
  Il est quatre heures moins le quart   *It is quarter to 4*
  Il est sept heures moins dix   *It is 10 to 7*
  Il est une heure moins cinq   *It is 5 to 1*
  Il est midi/minuit   *It is midday/midnight*
  Il est midi cinq   *It is 5 past 12 (noon)*
  Il est minuit dix   *It is 10 past 12 (midnight)*
  Il est midi et demi   *It is half past 12 (noon)*
  Il est minuit et demi   *It is half past 12 (midnight)*
  Il est vingt heures   *20:00*
  Il est vingt heures quinze   *20:15*
  Il est vingt heures trente   *20:30*
  Il est vingt heures quarante-cinq   *20:45*

Numbers, Time and Dates   *French Grammar*

DAYS OF THE WEEK (LES JOURS DE LA SEMAINE)

lundi	mardi	mercredi	jeudi	vendredi	samedi	dimanche
Monday	*Tuesday*	*Wednesday*	*Thursday*	*Friday*	*Saturday*	*Sunday*

Please remember:
1. No capital letters are used with days of the week or months of the year.
2. me<u>rcr</u>edi has two r's!!

MONTHS OF THE YEAR (LES MOIS DE L'AN)

janvier	février	mars	avril	mai	juin
January	*February*	*March*	*April*	*May*	*June*

juillet	août	septembre	octobre	novembre	décembre
July	*August*	*September*	*October*	*November*	*December*

Again, please remember:
    No capital letters are used with days of the week or months of the year.

DATES (LA DATE)

When writing/saying the date in French, you use cardinal numbers for all dates except the first of the month which has the ordinal: **premier**

    C'est aujourd'hui:-   le **premier** septembre
                                        le deux mars
                                        le quatre juillet
                                        le onze mai
    Mon anniversaire est le trente novembre
                                        le quinze février
                                        le vingt-cinq mai
                                        le vingt et un décembre

Il est **né** en dix-neuf cent quatre-vingt neuf   *He was born in 1989*
Elle est **née** en dix-neuf cent soixante-trois   *She was born in 1963*

Special days of the year (Les fêtes)

Le Jour de l'an	*New Year's Day*
Le Jour de Pâques	*Easter Sunday*
Le Jour de la Pentecôte	*Whit Sunday*
La Toussaint	*November 1st, All Saints*
La veille de Noël	*Christmas Eve*
Le Jour de Noël	*Christmas Day*
La Pâque	*Passover*
Le Nouvel An juif	*Rosh Hashanah*
Le Ramadan	*Ramadan*

French Grammar   *Numbers, Time and Dates*

How to translate:

   in

      *I get up at 7 **in** the morning*
      Je me lève à 7 heures **du** matin
      Le matin, je me lève à 7 heures

      *I come home at 6 o'clock **in** the evening*
      Je rentre à 6 heures **du** soir
      Le soir, je rentre à 6 heures

      ***In** the afternoon, I go to the library*
      L'après-midi, je vais à la bibliothèque

      *at 8 am/at 8 o'clock **in** the morning*
      à huit heures **du** matin

      *at 2 pm/at 2 o'clock **in** the afternoon*
      à deux heures **de l'**après-midi

      *at 6 pm/at 6 o'clock **in** the evening*
      à six heures **du** soir

      *We are leaving **in** an hour*
      Nous partons **dans** une heure

   for

      *I stayed there **for** 3 weeks*
      J'y suis resté **pendant** trois semaines

      *She will be in Paris **for** three days*
      Elle sera à Paris **pour** trois jours

      *She has been living in Paris **for** a year*
      Elle habite (à) Paris **depuis** un an
      (See page 57 on Special constructions using the present tense)

   ago

      *three days **ago***
      il y a trois jours

      *a long time **ago***
      il y a longtemps

PREPOSITIONS (LES PREPOSITIONS)

Here are some of the most widely used prepositions:

à:

Il va **à** Paris	*He is going **to** Paris*
Il est **à** Paris	*He is **in** Paris*
C'est **à** qui?	*Whose is it?*
C'est **à** moi!	*It's mine!*
à gauche	***on** the left*
à pied	***on** foot*
à voix basse	***in** a low voice*
à mon arrivée	*When I arrive(d), **on** my arrival*
Je pense **à** toi	*I'm thinking **about** you*
une tasse **à** thé	*a teacup (a cup for tea)*
à mon avis	*in my opinion*
au collège, **aux** magasins	***to/at** school, **to/at the** shops*
à l'église	***in/at** church, **to/at** the church*
à la piscine	***to/in/at** the swimming pool*
du matin **au** soir	*from morning **till** evening*
au printemps	***in** spring*

Remember that **au, à la, à l', aux** are also used in descriptions to translate the words **with, in**:

le garçon **au** pullover gris	*the boy **in** the grey pullover*
un homme **à la** barbe noire	*a man **with** a black beard*
une menthe **à l'**eau	*a mint cordial*
une femme **aux** yeux bleus	*a woman **with** blue eyes*

après:

La poste est **après** la banque	*The post office is **after** the bank*
après le déjeuner	***after** lunch*
Après avoir fini le travail ...	***After** finishing work ...*
Après être arrivée, elle ...	***After** she arrived, she ...*

au-dessus de:

Le bureau est **au-dessus du** restaurant	*The office is **over** the restaurant*

au sujet de:

Je lui ai écrit **au sujet de** ta visite	*I wrote to him **about** your visit*

autour de:

Il regardait **autour de** lui	*He was looking **about** him*
autour de la pièce	***around** the room*
une haie **autour de** la maison	*a hedge **round** the house*

French Grammar   *Prepositions*

à travers:
     ... **à travers** champs   ... *across the fields*

avant:
     avant midi   *before midday*
     avant le retour de son père   *before his father came/comes home*
     Il est arrivé **avant** nous   *He arrived before us*
     avant deux jours   *within two days*
     avant de partir, il ...   *Before leaving, he ...*
     avant tout   *above all*
     en 100 **avant** Jésus Christ   *in 100 BC*

avec:
     Il vient **avec** moi   *He comes/is coming with me*
     Et **avec** ça?   *Is there anything else?*
     Il l'a coupé **avec** des ciseaux   *He cut it with scissors*

chez:
     chez moi   *at my house/at home*
     chez le pâtissier   *at the cake shop*

dans:
     Il joue **dans** le jardin   *He is playing in the garden*
     Il posa le livre **dans** le tiroir   *He put the book in the drawer*
     Il a pris les livres **dans** le tiroir   *He took the books out of the drawer*
     Elle entre **dans** la maison   *She goes/is going into the house*

de:
     une tasse **de** thé   *a cup of tea*
     la voiture **de** Paul   *Paul's car*
     La terre est couverte **de** neige   *The ground is covered with snow*
     Le sac est plein **de** livres   *The bag is full of books*
     Le sac est plein **d'**argent   *The bag is full of money*
     Que penses-tu **d'**elle?   *What do you think of her?*
              (= *What is your opinion of her?*)

     d'une voix forte   *in a loud voice*
     une tête **de** garçon   *a boy's head*
     au mois **de** décembre   *in December*
     les vacances **de** Pâques   *the Easter holidays*
     plus **de** trois mille euros   *more than 3000 euros*

depuis:
     depuis hier   *since yesterday*
     Depuis quand attends-tu là?   *How long have you been waiting there?*
     J'habite Malvern **depuis** cinq ans   *I've been living in Malvern for five years*
     (see pages 51 and 57)

derrière:
    derrière l'hôtel — ***behind*** *the hotel*

dès:
    Dès demain j'y serai à huit heures — ***From*** *tomorrow, I'll be there at eight o'clock*
    Dès maintenant … — ***From*** *now on …*

devant:
    Il est **devant** la maison — *He is **in front of** the house*
    On se voit **devant** le cinéma? — *Shall we meet **outside** the cinema?*

en:
    Je vais **en** France — *I'm going **to** France*
    Je suis **en** France — *I am **in** France*
    en automne — ***in*** *autumn*
    en l'an 2003 — ***in*** *2003*
    Il arrive **en** voiture — *He comes **by** car*
    de temps **en** temps — ***from*** *time to time*
    un sac **en** cuir — *a leather bag (made of leather)*
    Elle a 10 euros **en** poche — *She has 10 euros **in** her pocket*

entre:
    La banque est **entre** la pharmacie et la boulangerie — *The bank is **between** the chemist's and the baker's*
    Entre nous … — ***Between*** *ourselves …*
    Vous êtes **entre** amis — *You are **among** friends*
    Le dîner est servi **entre** 20 heures et 22 heures — *Dinner is served **between** 8-10 pm*

hors (de):
    hors toi … — ***apart from/except for*** *you …*
    hors de danger — ***out of*** *danger*
    Il est **hors de** lui — *He is **beside** himself*

jusqu'à: (place)
    jusqu'à la banque — *as far as the bank*
    jusqu'au rondpoint — *as far as the roundabout*
    jusqu'aux feux — *as far as the lights*

jusqu'à: (time)
    jusqu'à minuit — *up to midnight*

le long de:
    Je marchais **le long de** la rue/ **le long du** couloir — *I was walking **along** the street/ **along** the corridor*

par:

Par ici, monsieur	*This way, Sir*
C'est **par** là	*It's that way*
par politesse	*out of politeness*
par un beau jour d'été	*on a fine summer day*
J'ai regardé **par** la fenêtre	*I looked out of the window*
Elle est assise **par** terre	*She's sitting on the ground*
Il arrive **par** le train	*He is coming by train*
deux fois **par** semaine	*twice a week*
cinq cours **par** jour	*five lessons a day*
deux **par** deux	*two by two*
Trente divisé **par** deux ...	*30 divided by 2 ...*
J'ai commencé **par** rire mais j'ai fini **par** pleurer	*I started by laughing, but ended up crying*
Il était blessé **par** une voiture	*He was injured by a car*

par-dessus:

Il a sauté **par-dessus** la haie	*He jumped over the hedge*

parmi:

Il était **parmi** les arbres	*He was among the trees*
Elle se tenait **parmi** les enfants	*She was standing among the children*
parmi la foule	*in the crowd*

pendant:

Il travaille **pendant** la matinée	*He works during the morning*
Elle siffle **pendant** des heures	*She whistles for hours*

à peu près:

Il mesure 1m 70 **à peu près**	*He is about 1 metre 70 tall*

pour:

C'est **pour** toi	*It's for you*
Je pars **pour** la Grèce demain	*I leave for Greece tomorrow*
Tu en as **pour** dix minutes de marche	*It will take you ten minutes to walk there*
Il est **pour** Nantes FC	*He's a Nantes supporter*

près de:

Est-ce qu'il y a un café **près d'**ici?	*Is there a café nearby?*
La voiture est **près de** la maison	*The car is near the house*
Elle s'assied **près de** moi	*She sits down near me*
Près de 50 élèves sont partis hier	*Almost 50 pupils left yesterday*

quant à:

Quant à moi, je reste ici	*As for me, I'm staying here*

Prepositions   *French Grammar*

sans:
    sans bagages — *without any luggage*
    Il est sorti **sans** rien dire — *He went out **without** saying anything*
    Elle sort **sans** mot dire — *She goes out **without** a word*

sous:
    Le chien est **sous** la table — *The dog is **under** the table*
    On a fait la visite du château **sous** la pluie — *We visited the castle **in** the rain*

sur:
    Les tasses sont **sur** la table — *The cups are **on** the table*
    La fenêtre donne **sur** le jardin — *The window looks **out on** the garden*
    9 fois **sur** 10 — *9 times **out of** 10*
    Il a 12 **sur** 20 — *He has 12 **out of** 20*
    Une personne **sur** cinq — *One **in** five people*
    Travaux **sur** 10km — *Road works **for** 10km*
    Virages **sur** 2km — *Bends **for** 2km*
    Il prend la pomme **sur** la table — *He takes the apple **off** the table*
    Il pleut **sur** Londres — *It is raining **in** London*

vers:
    Il marche **vers** l'église — *He walks **towards** the church*
    vers le nord — ***towards/facing** the north*
    vers la fin de la semaine — ***towards** the end of the week*
    Elle se retourne **vers** moi — *She turns **towards** me*
    Il viendra **vers** 9 heures — *He'll be here **about** 9 o'clock*

but:
    Il est cruel **envers** son chat — *He is cruel **to** his cat*
    Son attitude **envers** ses amis — *His attitude **towards** his friends*

French Grammar *Pronouns*

PRONOUNS (LES PRONOMS)

SUBJECT PRONOUNS (LES PRONOMS PERSONNELS - SUJET)

There are nine of these:

je	tu	il	elle	on	nous	vous	ils	elles
I	*you*	*he*	*she*	*one*	*we*	*you*	*they (m)*	*they (f)*

When using these pronouns remember that:

1. **Tu** is used when speaking to **one person** you know well, to a member of the family, to a child or to a pet.

2. **Vous** is used when speaking to one adult you do not know very well.
   Vous is also always used for speaking to two or more people.

3. **Il** and **elle** can mean *it* when referring to masculine or feminine nouns.

4. **On** has a variety of meanings: *we, one, they, you, people, someone*:
   Example:
   On est allé à la plage
   We went to the beach
   On est obligé de porter l'uniforme scolaire
   One has to wear school uniform
   On n'accepte pas les cartes de crédit chez Dominique
   They don't accept credit cards at Dominique's
   Note also:
   Ici **on** parle anglais
   English spoken here (see page 74)

5. **Ils** is used for *they* when:

   a) all the nouns referred to are masculine
   Example:
   Les garçons? Oui, **ils** sont là-bas
   The boys? Yes, they are over there

   b) there is a group of nouns, **one** of which is masculine
   Example:
   Marie, Louise et Yves? Oui, **ils** sont dans le jardin
   Marie, Louise and Yves? Yes, they are in the garden

6. **Elles** is used for *they* when all the nouns are feminine:
   Example:
   Les trois filles? **Elles** sont à la maison
   The three girls? They are at home
   Où sont Maman et Laure? **Elles** viennent d'arriver
   Where are Mother and Laura? They have just arrived

Pronouns   *French Grammar*

OBJECT PRONOUNS (LES PRONOMS PERSONNELS)

There are two types of object pronoun: direct and indirect

Direct:

me	te	se	le	la	nous	vous	les
me	*you*	*himself*	*him*	*her*	*us*	*you*	*them*
		herself	*it*	*it*			
		oneself					
		itself					

These are used when the thing or person is the direct recipient of the verb action:
Example:
Il **me** voit	*He sees **me***
Je **les** achète	*I buy **them***
Elle **nous** regarde	*She is watching **us***
Vous ne **les** voyez pas	*You do not/cannot see **them***

Indirect: These pronouns express the Genitive and Dative ideas *of, to* and *for*

me	*of, to, for me*
te	*of, to, for you*
se	*of, to, for himself, herself, itself, oneself (reflexive)*
lui	*of, to, for him, her*
nous	*of, to, for us*
vous	*of, to, for you*
leur	*of, to, for them*

Example:
Il **me** parle	*He speaks **to me***
Il **se** brosse les cheveux	*He brushes his hair*
Tu **lui** donnes de l'argent	*You give **him/her** (= to him/her) some money*
Nous **leur** disons "Bonjour"	*We say "Good Morning" **to them***
Vous **m'**avez téléphoné	*You phoned **me***
Ils **vous** offrent un cadeau	*They give **you** (= to you) a present*

There are two other pronouns to remember in this group:

y   which means *there, to it*:
       Example: J'**y** habite   *I live **there***

en   which means *of it, of them, some, any, from it, from them*:
       Example: As-tu de l'argent? Oui j'**en** ai
                         *Have you any money? Yes, I have **some***
                         Vous m'**en** avez déjà parlé
                         *You have already spoken to me **about it***

En is usually used for things.
For people and animals it is customary to use **de lui, d'elle, d'eux, d'elles**

       Example: Je me souviens **de lui/d'elle/d'eux/d'elles**
                         *I remember **him/her/them/them***

French Grammar *Pronouns*

POSITION OF PRONOUNS (OÙ METTRE LES PRONOMS PERSONNELS?)

Having decided which pronoun you need, the next consideration is its position in the sentence.

In sentences with simple (single word) tenses like the present, future, imperfect, conditional and past historic, the pronouns come immediately before the verb.

    Example: Je **le** vois   *I see **him/it***
                   Il **me** parlera   *He will speak **to me***
                   Elle **la** cherchait   *She was looking for **it/her***
                   Nous **les** aurions   *We would have **them***
                   Il **les** acheta   *He bought **them***

In sentences with compound tenses like the perfect, pluperfect, etc, the pronouns come before the auxiliary verb:

    Example: Je **vous** ai vu   *I saw **you***
                   Elle **lui** avait parlé   *She had spoken **to him/her***
                 Il **y** est allé   *He went **there***

Exception to this position rule:

If you are telling someone to do something, that is, using the verb in the imperative, then the pronoun follows its verb and is joined to it with a hyphen:

    Example: Regardez-**le**!   *Look at **him/it**!*
                   Donnez-**lui** l'argent!   *Give **him/her** the money!*

Remember that **me** becomes **moi** and **te** becomes **toi** in this type of sentence:

    Example: Donnez-**moi** le livre!   *Give **me** the book*
                   Assieds-**toi**!   *Sit down*

But

If the command is negative, that is, if you are telling someone **not** to do something, then the pronoun comes **before** the verb:

    Example: Ne **le** regardez pas   *Don't look at **him/it***
                   Ne **me** donnez pas le livre   *Don't give **me** the book*
                 Ne **t'**assieds pas par terre   *Don't sit down on the ground*
                 (note: **moi** is now **me** again and **toi** is now **te** again)

Pronouns   French Grammar

ORDER OF PRONOUNS (TABLEAU DES PRONOMS PERSONNELS)

If you have more than one pronoun in a sentence, the order can be set out in table form as follows and you can pick one from each column.

1	2	3	4	5	6	7	8	9
je	ne	me					VERB	pas
tu	ne	te					VERB	pas
il	ne	se	le	lui			VERB	pas
elle	ne	se	la	lui	y	en	VERB	pas
nous	ne	nous					VERB	pas
vous	ne	vous	les	leur			VERB	pas
ils	ne	se	les	leur			VERB	pas
elles	ne	se					VERB	pas

Example:
    Je ne **le lui** donne pas   *I do not give it to him/her*
    (1 + 2 + 4 + 5 + 8 + 9)
    Elle **nous en** offre   *She offers some to us*
    (1 + 3 +7 + 8)
    Ils **nous le** donnent   *They give it to us*
    (1 + 3 + 4 + 8)

EMPHATIC, STRESSED OR DISJUNCTIVE PRONOUNS (LES FORMES ACCENTUÉES)

They are:

moi	**toi**	**lui**	**elle**	**nous**	**vous**	**eux**	**elles**
me	*you*	*him*	*her*	*us*	*you*	*them (m)*	*them (f)*

They are used:
1. With c'est and ce sont
    Example: C'est **moi**, ce sont **eux**
                It's me, it's them

2. After prepositions
    Example: avec **lui**, pour **elle**, sans **moi**
                with him, for her, without me

3. To emphasize the subject pronoun
    Example: **Moi**, j'aime la musique classique, mais **lui**, il préfère le jazz
                I like classical music, but he prefers jazz

4. As a one-word answer to a question
    Example: Qui a jeté ce sac? **Lui**!
                Who threw that bag? He did!

5. When making comparisons
    Example: Mon frère est plus petit que **moi**
                *My brother is smaller than **I am**/than **me***

French Grammar *Pronouns*

6. In composite subjects
   Example: **Vous et moi**, nous y irons demain
   You and I will go there tomorrow

7. When combined with **-même**
   Example: Je l'ai écrit **moi-même**   *I wrote it **myself***
   Il l'a dit **lui-même**   *He said it **himself***

8. For use with **on** there is **soi-même**
   Example: On doit le faire **soi-même**   *One must do it **oneself***

RELATIVE PRONOUNS (LES PRONOMS RELATIFS)

These are **qui, que, qu', à qui** and **dont**

They are used to introduce a clause which is giving more information about a noun. You must select the correct relative pronoun according to its grammatical function within the clause.

1. When the relative pronoun is the subject of the clause, use **qui**:

   Example: La dame **qui** chante est ma tante
   *The lady **who** is singing is my aunt*
   Les gants **qui** sont sur la table sont à moi
   The gloves on the table are mine

   Remember that **qui** is never abbreviated.

2. When the relative pronoun is the object of the verb, use **que**, or **qu'** if the next word begins with a vowel.
   Note that clauses of this type will contain a different subject in the form of a noun or pronoun.

   Example: Le travail **que** je fais est difficile
   The work I am doing is hard
   Les fleurs **que** j'ai achet**ées**
   The flowers I bought

   Notice that in sentences with the verb in the perfect or pluperfect tense, the past participle will normally show agreement with the direct object because the direct object precedes the verb (see page 60).

3. When the relative pronoun is the indirect object of the clause, use
   à qui/avec qui/après qui when referring to people:

   Example: Voici la dame **à qui** j'ai donné la carte
   Here is the lady to whom I gave the map
   Voilà l'homme **avec qui** je parlais
   There is the man I was talking to

45

4. When the pronoun means *whose, of which, of whom,* use **dont** if referring to things.

> Example: le film **dont** je te parlais
> *the film I was telling you about*
> la maison **dont** toutes les fenêtres sont fermées
> *the house with all the windows closed*

5. **Ce qui, ce que** are also forms of the relative pronoun.
They mean *what* (= that which).
The correct form to choose is again governed by its grammatical function in the sentence.

> Example: Je voudrais voir **ce qui** va arriver (subject)
> *I'd like to see what will happen*
> Je voudrais voir **ce que** vous faites (object)
> *I would like to see what you are doing*

Sometimes the word **tout** is added to them:

> Example: **Tout ce qui** brille n'est pas or (subject)
> *All that glitters is not gold*
> Il a compris **tout ce que** j'ai dit (object)
> *He understood everything I said*

6. **Lequel, laquelle, lesquels, lesquelles** meaning *which* are used as relative pronouns after prepositions. Remember that you must choose your pronoun according to the gender of the noun to which it refers.

> Example: le crayon **avec lequel** il dessinait
> *the pencil with which he was drawing*
> la voiture **dans laquelle** elle était assise
> *the car in which she was sitting*

Four things to notice here:

(i) When linked with **à**, these pronouns change their forms to **auquel, à laquelle, auxquels, auxquelles**

> Example: un problème **auquel** il n'avait pas pensé
> *a problem he had not thought of*

(ii) When linked with **de**, these pronouns change their forms to **duquel, de laquelle, desquels, desquelles**.

> Example: le musée à côté **duquel** se trouve la banque
> *the museum next to which is the bank*

(iii) *In which/on which* can often be more easily translated as **où**:

   Example: La ville **où** j'habite s'appelle Malvern
   *The town **where** I live is called Malvern*

(iv) With **parmi**, however, **lesquels** and **lesquelles** can be used for people and things:

   Example: Les enfants **parmi lesquels** il se tenait
   *The children **among whom** he was standing*
   Les fleurs **parmi lesquelles** il se tenait
   *The flowers **among which** he was standing*

INTERROGATIVE PRONOUNS (LES PRONOMS INTERROGATIFS)

These pronouns ask questions: *who, what, which one?*

When talking about **people**:

   If the word *who?* is the subject of the verb, you use either **qui?** or **qui est-ce qui?**

   Example: **Qui** arrive? **Qui est-ce qui** arrive? *Who is coming?*

   If the pronoun is the object of the verb you use **qui?** or **qui est-ce que?**

   Example: **Qui est-ce que** vous voyez?   *Who (Whom) can you see?*

   If the pronoun is used with prepositions you use **qui**

   Example: **A qui** parles-tu?   *Who are you talking **to**?*
   Avec qui êtes-vous allé?   *Who did you go **with**?*
   De qui parles-tu?   *Who are you talking **about**?*

When talking about **things**:

   If the word *what?* is the subject of the verb, you use **Qu'est-ce qui?**

   Example: **Qu'est-ce qui** vous intéresse? *What interests you?*

   If *what* is the object of the verb you use **que** or **qu'** and invert the verb, or **qu'est-ce que** and leave the verb in its normal order.

   Example: **Que** fais-tu là?   *What are you doing?*
   Qu'est-ce que tu me racontes?   *What are you telling me?*

   If *what* is used with a preposition you choose **quoi**.

   Example: **A quoi** penses-tu?   *What are you thinking **of**?*
   De quoi parlent-ils?   *What are they talking **about**?*
   Avec quoi vas-tu allumer le feu? *What will you use to light the fire?*

Pronouns   *French Grammar*

When asking **which one(s)**, use **lequel, laquelle, lesquels** and **lesquelles** for both **people** and **things**.

    Example: "J'ai vu une de tes amies hier." "Ah oui? **Laquelle?**"
               *"I saw one of your friends yesterday." "Oh yes, **which one?**"*
               Lequel de ces deux anoraks est à toi?
               ***Which** of these two anoraks belongs to you?*
               As-tu acheté les cartes-postales? - **Lesquelles?**
               *Did you buy the postcards? - **Which ones?***

DEMONSTRATIVE PRONOUNS (LES PRONOMS DÉMONSTRATIFS)

These include:
1.   **ce, ceci,** *(this)* **cela, ça,** *(that)*
        Example: Regardez **ceci!**   *Look at **this!***
                   As-tu vu **cela?**   *Did you see **that?***
                   Ne fais pas **ça!**   *Don't do **that!***
                   (**ça** is the shortened form of **cela**)
    Notice that **ce** is shortened to **c'** when it is followed by another vowel:
        Example: **C'**est un garçon   *He is a boy*
        but: **Ce** sont mes meilleurs amis   *These are my best friends*

2.   **Celui, celle, ceux, celles** *(this, these, the one(s) which)* agree with the gender and number of the noun to which they refer.
    They are usually followed by **qui/que** or **de**:

        Example: Quel arbre? **Celui qui** est près de la maison
                  *Which tree? **The one** near the house*
                  Quelle voiture? **Celle qui** est devant le garage
                  *Which car? **The one** in front of the garage*
                  Quels livres? **Ceux que** je t'ai montrés hier
                  *Which books? **The ones** I showed you yesterday*
                  Quelles robes? **Celles que** j'ai mises dans l'armoire
                  *Which dresses? **The ones** I put in the wardrobe*

    When followed by **de** they mean "the one(s) belonging to"

        Example: Quel anorak? **Celui de** mon frère
                  Which anorak? My brother's
                  Quels crayons? **Ceux de** ma sœur
                  Which pencils? My sister's

    They can be used with **-ci** or **-là** added to give greater emphasis:

        Example: "Quelle maison? **Celle-ci?**"   "Mais non! **Celle-là**"
                  *"Which house? **This** one?"*   *"No, **that** one!"*

French Grammar   *Pronouns*

POSSESSIVE PRONOUNS (LES PRONOMS POSSESSIFS)

These are the words which mean *mine, yours, his, hers, its, ours, yours, theirs*.

There are three or four forms for each:

masc sing	fem sing	masc pl	fem pl	Meaning
one owner, one object owned		*one owner, several objects owned*		
le mien	la mienne	les miens	les miennes	*mine*
le tien	la tienne	les tiens	les tiennes	*yours*
le vôtre	la vôtre	les vôtres	les vôtres	*yours*
le sien	la sienne	les siens	les siennes	*his/its*
le sien	la sienne	les siens	les siennes	*hers/its*
2+ owners, one object owned		*2+ owners, several objects owned*		
le nôtre	la nôtre	les nôtres	les nôtres	*ours*
le vôtre	la vôtre	les vôtres	les vôtres	*yours*
le leur	la leur	les leurs	les leurs	*theirs*

The form used will vary according to the gender and number of the noun referred to. **Choice of gender depends on the gender of the object owned, not the sex of the owner:**

Example: "Voici mon sac! Où est **le tien**?" a-t-elle dit
                   "Here's my bag. Where is yours?" she said
                  Il préfère ma voiture à **la tienne**
                  He prefers my car to yours

INDEFINITE PRONOUNS (LES PRONOMS INDÉFINIS)

Here are some of the most common indefinite pronouns, together with examples of how to use them:

autre: Où as-tu mis les **autres**?
*Where did you put the **others**?*

chacun/chacune: **chacun** des garçons, **chacune** des filles
***each** of the boys, **each** of the girls*

n'importe can be used with various other words to mean *any ... at all*

n'importe qui	*anybody at all*
n'importe lequel	*no matter which*
n'importe quoi	*anything at all*
n'importe où	*anywhere*
n'importe comment	*anyhow*

plusieurs: Est-ce qu'il a des jeux électroniques? Oui, il en a **plusieurs**
*Has he got any video games? Yes, he's got **several***

quelqu'un: J'attends **quelqu'un**
*I'm waiting for **someone***

quelques-uns/unes: **Quelques-unes** de ces photos sont jolies
***Some** of these photos are pretty*

tout: J'ai **tout** vu
*I saw **everything***
Elle voulait **tout** savoir
*She wanted to know **everything***

tous/toutes: Elle nous voit **tous/toutes**
*She sees us **all***
tous would be used if the group is all male or mixed;
toutes would be used for an all-female group.
(Note that when **tous** is a pronoun the **-s** is sounded.)

tous/toutes les deux Ils étaient grands, **tous les deux**
*They were **both** big (m)*
Elles étaient petites, **toutes les deux**
*They were **both** small (f)*

tout le monde *(everybody)*

Example: Remember that this pronoun takes a **singular** verb.
Tout le monde **était** là
Everyone was there

VERBS (LES VERBES)

PRESENT TENSE (LE PRÉSENT)

Use of the present tense (L'emploi du présent)
This is the tense which is used to talk and write about:
- events which are taking place at this moment in time
- events which take place regularly
- events in the near future which are certain

The present tense is also used:
- after **depuis**
- after **voilà** and **il y a** in time idioms
- with **venir de**

Notice that there are **three** forms of the present tense in English but only **one** in French:
I go, I am going, I do go: - all these are translated by **je vais**
He watches, he is watching, he does watch: - all these are expressed by **il regarde**

Never try to put in a word for *am, is, are* or *does* in these circumstances - they are already included in the verb form.

Formation of the present tense (La formation du présent)

Regular verbs
Regular verbs in French can be recognised by the last two letters of their infinitive:
    travail**ler**   fin**ir**   répon**dre**
These letters give the clue to the pattern the verbs will follow in various tenses.

Present tense of -er verbs
The largest family of regular verbs is the **-er** group.
To form the present tense of an **-er** verb, for example travailler, take away the final **-er**, then add the endings **-e, -es, -e, -ons, -ez, -ent**.

Travailler - *to work*

je travaill**e**	*I work, I am working, I do work*
tu travaill**es**	*you work, you are working, you do work*
il travaill**e**	*he works, he is working, he does work*
elle travaill**e**	*she works, she is working, she does work*
on travaill**e**	*one works, one is working, one does work*
Chris travaill**e**	*Chris works, Chris is working, Chris does work*
nous travaill**ons**	*we work, we are working, we do work*
vous travaill**ez**	*you work, you are working, you do work*
ils travaill**ent**	*they work, they are working, they do work*
elles travaill**ent**	*they work, they are working, they do work*
les enfants travaill**ent**	*the children work, are working, do work*

Verbs   ***French Grammar***

Other common regular -er verbs include:
    aider, aimer, arriver*, chercher, compter, danser, déjeuner, désirer, dessiner, détester, donner, durer, écouter, entrer*, fumer, gagner, inviter, jouer, laver, louer, marcher, monter*, montrer, oublier, parler, penser, pleurer, porter, poser, pousser, préparer, quitter, raconter, regarder, rencontrer, rentrer*, réparer, réserver, rester*, retourner*, rouler, sauter, sonner, tomber*, toucher, tourner, traverser, trouver, visiter, voler

        Verbs marked * take être in compound tenses.

Irregular -er verbs
The only really irregular verb with an infinitive ending in -er is
    aller - *to go*

je vais	*I go, I am going, I do go*
tu vas	*you go, you are going, you do go*
il/elle/on/Chris va	*he/she/one/Chris goes, is going, does go*
nous allons	*we go, we are going, we do go*
vous allez	*you go, you are going, you do go*
ils/elles vont	*they go, they are going, they do go*
les enfants vont	*the children go, are going, do go*

Some frequently used -er verbs have slight variations to the usual present tense pattern:
The reason for these changes is that there are hard vowels (-a, -o, -u) and soft vowels (-i, -e and -y) in French.

c is pronounced as a hard **k** in front of hard vowels and **ss** in front of soft vowels:
    Example: **commencer** (shows both pronunciations)

g is pronounced as a hard **g** in front of hard vowels and **je** in front of soft vowels:
    Example: **ga**rder (hard)   man**ge**r (soft)

To soften a hard sound use **-e** after the consonant and to harden a soft vowel use **u**:
    Example: nous mang**e**ons (soft)
                    long (m), long**u**e (f) (hard)

1.   **Voyager** and other verbs ending in **-ger** have an additional **-e** before **-ons** in the **nous** form to make the **g** soft in front of the **–o**.

je voyage	nous voyag**e**ons
tu voyages	vous voyagez
il voyage	ils voyagent
elle voyage	elles voyagent
on voyage	les enfants voyagent
Chris voyage	

Other verbs of this type are:
    changer, échanger, loger, manger, nager, obliger, partager, ranger

French Grammar *Verbs*

2. **Commencer** and other verbs ending in **-cer** make the **c** soft by giving it a cedilla in places where the **c** is followed by **-a** or **-o**.

    je commence   nous commen**ç**ons
    tu commences   vous commencez
    il commence   ils commencent
    elle commence   elles commencent
    on commence   les enfants commencent
    Chris commence

Other verbs of this type are:
    avancer, lancer, menacer, placer, prononcer, remplacer

Other -er verbs make different changes where there are silent endings:

1. **S'appeler*** doubles the **-l** where the ending is silent.

    je m'appelle   nous nous appelons
    tu t'appelles   vous vous appelez
    il s'appelle   ils s'appellent
    elle s'appelle   elles s'appellent
    on s'appelle   les enfants s'appellent
    Comment s'appelle-t-il?

Non-reflexive appeler also follows this pattern.

2. **Jeter** doubles the **-t** where the ending is silent.

    je jette   nous jetons
    tu jettes   vous jetez
    il jette   ils jettent
    elle jette   elles jettent
    on jette   les enfants jettent
    Chris jette

3. Verbs like **se promener*** add accents when the ending is silent.

    je me promène   nous nous promenons
    tu te promènes   vous vous promenez
    il se promène   ils se promènent
    elle se promène   elles se promènent
    on se promène   les enfants se promènent
    Chris se promène

Other verbs of this type are:
    acheter, geler, lever, se lever*, mener, peser

4. Verbs like **préférer** change the accent pattern for a silent ending.

je préfère	nous préférons
tu préfères	vous préférez
il préfère	ils préfèrent
elle préfère	elles préfèrent
on préfère	les enfants préfèrent
Chris préfère	

Other verbs of this type are:
espérer, s'inquiéter*, répéter, révéler

5. Verbs whose infinitive ends in **-yer,** such as **envoyer** change the **-y** to an **-i** where the ending is silent.

j'envoie	nous envoyons
tu envoies	vous envoyez
il envoie	ils envoient
elle envoie	elles envoient
on envoie	les enfants envoient
Chris envoie	

Other verbs of this type are:
appuyer, balayer, employer, ennuyer, s'ennuyer*, essayer, essuyer, nettoyer, payer

Present Tense of -ir Verbs

Two much smaller families of regular verbs are the two **-ir** groups of verbs.

Group 1
To form the present tense of the first group take away the final **-ir** from the infinitive, then add the endings **-is, -is, -it, -issons, -issez, -issent.**

Finir - *to finish*

je fin**is**	*I finish, I am finishing, I do finish*
tu fin**is**	*you finish, you are finishing, you do finish*
il fin**it**	*he finishes, he is finishing, he does finish*
elle fin**it**	*she finishes, she is finishing, she does finish*
on fin**it**	*one finishes, one is finishing, one does finish*
Chris fin**it**	*Chris finishes, is finishing, does finish*
nous fin**issons**	*we finish, we are finishing, we do finish*
vous fin**issez**	*you finish, you are finishing, you do finish*
ils fin**issent**	*they finish, they are finishing, they do finish*
elles fin**issent**	*they finish, they are finishing, they do finish*
les enfants fin**issent**	*the children finish, are finishing, do finish*

Other common regular Group 1 -ir verbs are:
agrandir, applaudir, atterrir(*), bâtir, choisir, démolir, grandir, remplir, rougir

Group 2
Some commonly used **-ir** verbs have variations in their present tense. They behave like an **-er** verb present tense:

Ouvrir - *to open*

j'ouvre	nous ouvr**ons**
tu ouvr**es**	vous ouvr**ez**
il ouvre	ils ouvr**ent**
elle ouvre	elles ouvr**ent**
on ouvre	les enfants ouvr**ent**
Chris ouvre	

Other Group 2 -ir verbs are:
couvrir, découvrir, offrir, recouvrir, souffrir

There are many irregular **-ir** verbs, and those listed here may be found in the Verb Table (pages 88-106):

acceuillir, bouillir, contenir, courir, ceuillir, devenir*, dormir, s'endormir*, entretenir, fuir, maintenir, mentir, mourir*, obtenir, parcourir, partir*, parvenir*, prévenir, repartir*, ressentir, retenir, revenir*, sentir, se sentir*, servir, se servir*, sortir*, soutenir, se souvenir*, survenir*, tenir, venir*

Verbs marked * take être in compound tenses.

Present Tense of -re Verbs

The third family of regular verbs is the **-re** group.

To form the present tense of an **-re** verb, take away the final **-re** from the infinitive and add the endings: **-s, -s, -, -ons, -ez, -ent.**

Répondre - *to answer*

je répond**s**	*I answer, I am answering, I do answer*
tu répond**s**	*you answer, you are answering, you do answer*
il répond	*he answers, he is answering, he does answer*
elle répond	*she answers, she is answering, she does answer*
on répond	*one answers, one is answering, one does answer*
Chris répond	*Chris answers, is answering, does answer*
nous répond**ons**	*we answer, we are answering, we do answer*
vous répond**ez**	*you answer, you are answering, you do answer*
ils répond**ent**	*they answer, they are answering, they do answer*
elles répond**ent**	*they answer, they are answering, they do answer*
les enfants répond**ent**	*the children answer, are answering, do answer*

Other commonly used regular -re verbs are:

attendre, battre, descendre*, entendre, intrerrompre, pendre, rendre, rompre, vendre

Verbs marked * take être in compound tenses.

Irregular -re verbs

There are many irregular **-re** verbs, and those listed will be found in the Verb Table (pages 88-106):

apprendre, atteindre, boire, comprendre, conduire, connaître, construire, coudre, craindre, croire, décrire, détruire, dire, disparaître, dissoudre, écrire, éteindre, être, faire, inscrire, instruire, interdire, introduire, joindre, lire, mettre, naître*, paraître, peindre, se plaindre*, plaire, poursuivre, prendre, produire, promettre, reconnaître, réduire, refaire, rejoindre, relire, reprendre, rire, satisfaire, soumettre, souffrire, sourire, suivre, surprendre, survivre, se taire*, vaincre, vivre

Verbs marked * take être in compound tenses.

Present Tense of -oir Verbs

There is a fourth group of verbs - those whose infinitives end in **-oir**. They are all irregular and have to be learned individually, and those listed below are found in the Verb Table (pages 88-106):

s'asseoir*, avoir, devoir, falloir, pleuvoir, pouvoir, recevoir, savoir, voir, vouloir

Verbs marked * take être in compound tenses.

Present Tense of Reflexive Verbs

Reflexive verbs are those verbs which have **se** or **s'** in front of the infinitive: **se lever***, **s'habiller***, etc. The extra pronoun often shows that the object (the person receiving the action of the verb) is the same person as the subject (the person performing the action of the verb)

Example: Je **me** lave   *I wash (**myself**)*
           Elles **se** réveillent   *They wake up*

Se réveiller* - *to wake up*

je **me** réveille	*I wake up, I am waking up, I do wake up*
tu **te** réveilles	*you wake up, you are waking up, you do wake up*
il **se** réveille	*he wakes up, he is waking up, he does wake up*
elle **se** réveille	*she wakes up, she is waking up, she does wake up*
on **se** réveille	*one wakes up, one is waking up, one does wake up*
Chris **se** réveille	*Chris wakes up, is waking up, does wake up*
nous **nous** réveill**ons**	*we wake up, we are waking up, we do wake up*
vous **vous** réveill**ez**	*you wake up, you are waking up, you do wake up*
ils **se** réveill**ent**	*they wake up, they are waking up, they do wake*
elles **se** réveill**ent**	*they wake up, they are waking, they do wake up*
les enfants **se** réveill**ent**	*the children wake up, are waking, do wake up*

French Grammar *Verbs*

1. Notice that the reflexive pronoun is put between the subject pronoun and the verb.

    Example: Il **se** lave   *He washes* (***himself***)

2. Reflexive verbs are often used when referring to a part of the body. See page 61.

    Example: Je **me** brosse les cheveux   *I brush my hair*

3. Use the correct form of the reflexive pronouns for the person of the verb

    Example: je **me**, tu **te**, il/elle/on/Chris **se**,
    nous **nous**, vous **vous**, ils/elles/les enfants **se**

4. **Me, te, se** all contract to **m', t', s'** before a vowel or silent **h**.

    Example: Je **m'**habille   *I get dressed*

5. When the reflexive verb is used in its infinitive form, remember that the reflexive pronoun has to agree with the subject of the verb.
    Example: **Je** dois **me** lever de bonne heure demain matin
    I must get up early tomorrow morning
    Nous allons **nous** coucher à 10h 30
    We are going to go to bed at 10.30

Some of the most commonly used reflexive verbs are:

s'amuser*	*to have fun*	se faire* mal	*to hurt oneself*
s'appeler*	*to be called*	s'habiller*	*to get dressed*
s'approcher de*	*to approach*	s'intéresser* à	*to be interested in*
s'arrêter*	*to stop*	se mettre* à	*to begin to*
s'asseoir*	*to sit down*	se laver*	*to wash oneself*
se baigner*	*to bathe*	se lever*	*to get up*
se coucher*	*to go to bed*	se peigner*	*to comb one's hair*
se débrouiller*	*to manage*	se promener*	*to go for a walk*
se dépêcher*	*to hurry*	se raser*	*to shave*
se déshabiller*	*to undress*	se reposer*	*to rest*
se disputer* avec	*to quarrel with*	se sauver*	*to run away*
s'entendre* avec	*to agree with*	se sentir*	*to feel*
se fâcher*	*to get angry*	se trouver*	*to be situated*

Reflexive verbs all take être in the perfect tense and are marked *
See Verb Table for s'asseoir* and -**er** verb section for s'appeler*, se lever* and se promener*

Special Constructions using the present tense (des cas particuliers)

1. **depuis** - *for, since* uses a present tense in French to convey a meaning which, in English, seems to require a perfect tense. If the action started in the past but is still continuing, then you must use a present tense after **depuis**.

    Example: J'apprends le français **depuis** cinq ans
    I have been learning French for five years (and am still doing so)
    Il habite à Malvern **depuis** longtemps
    He has been living in Malvern for a long time (and still does)

Verbs   *French Grammar*

2. **venir de** - *to have just*
   The present tense of venir + de + infinitive means *to have just done something*.

   Example: Il vient de manger une pomme
                   He has just eaten an apple
                   Elle vient d'arriver
                   She has just arrived

3. **être en train de** - means being *in the process of* doing something.

   Example: Il est en train de faire ses devoirs
                   He is doing his homework
                   Je suis en train de lire un livre d'Astérix
                   I am reading an Astérix book at the moment

4. **être sur le point de** - *to be about to* - conveys the meaning of immediate future.

   Example: Je suis sur le point de sortir
                   I am just about to go out
                   Elle est sur le point d'acheter une voiture
                   She is going to buy a car
                   (= on the point of buying)

THE PERFECT TENSE (LE PASSÉ COMPOSÉ)

Use of the perfect tense (L'emploi du passé composé)
This is the tense which is used in **conversation** and in **letters** to describe:
- an action in the past which has been completed
- an action in the past which happened on one occasion only

Notice that, as with the present tense, there are several ways of expressing this verb form in English but only one form in French:
     I worked hard, I have worked hard, I have been working hard, I did work hard
are **all** expressed in French by **j'ai travaillé dur.**

Formation of the perfect tense (La formation du passé composé)
The perfect tense has two parts - the auxiliary verb (l'auxiliaire), which is the present tense of either **avoir** or **être** - and the past participle (le participe passé).
In English, past participles often end in **-ed -en,** or **-t** *(looked, hidden, bought)*

Perfect tense with avoir - regular verbs (L'auxiliaire 'avoir' et les verbes reguliers)

To form the past participles of regular verbs (including those **-er** verbs with variations in the spellings of the present tense) remove the final two letters (**-er, -ir, -re**) from the infinitive and add **-é, -i** or **-u** to the remaining stem.

                 travailler becomes **travaillé**
                 finir becomes **fini**
                 répondre becomes **répondu**

Then use the past participle with its auxiliary as follows:

j'ai travaillé	j'ai fini	j'ai répondu
tu as travaillé	tu as fini	tu as répondu
il a travaillé	il a fini	il a répondu
elle a travaillé	elle a fini	elle a répondu
on a travaillé	on a fini	on a répondu
nous avons travaillé	nous avons fini	nous avons répondu
vous avez travaillé	vous avez fini	vous avez répondu
ils ont travaillé	ils ont fini	ils ont répondu
elles ont travaillé	elles ont fini	elles ont répondu
les enfants ont travaillé	les enfants ont fini	les enfants ont répondu

When writing, you **must not** forget the accent on the **-er** past participle.

Perfect tense with avoir - irregular verbs ('avoir' et les verbes irréguliers)

Many of the most commonly used verbs are irregular in the perfect tense. They do, in fact, use the present tense of **avoir** as their auxiliary but their past participles are irregular in form and, as such, have to be learned individually:

Example: **voir** - (vu)   **ouvrir** - (ouvert)   **prendre** - (pris)

j'ai vu	j'ai ouvert	j'ai pris
tu as vu	tu as ouvert	tu as pris
il a vu	il a ouvert	il a pris
elle a vu	elle a ouvert	elle a pris
on a vu	on a ouvert	on a pris
nous avons vu	nous avons ouvert	nous avons pris
vous avez vu	vous avez ouvert	vous avez pris
ils ont vu	ils ont ouvert	ils ont pris
elles ont vu	elles ont ouvert	elles ont pris

Here is a list of the most common **avoir** verbs with their past participles (p.p.).

Infinitive	p.p.	Infinitive	p.p.	Infinitive	p.p.
avoir	eu	écrire	écrit	recevoir	reçu
boire	bu	être	été	rire	ri
comprendre	compris	faire	fait	savoir	su
conduire	conduit	lire	lu	tenir	tenu
connaître	connu	mettre	mis	vivre	vécu
courir	couru	ouvrir	ouvert	voir	vu
croire	cru	pleuvoir	plu	vouloir	voulu
devoir	dû	pouvoir	pu		
dire	dit	prendre	pris		

These must be **learned** thoroughly. They are all in the Verb Table (pages 88-106)

Verbs   *French Grammar*

Avoir and the PDO rule (L'auxiliaire 'avoir' et l'accord du participe passé)
The tenses in which this rule operates are compound tenses such as the perfect tense (passé composé). In a compound tense of any verb which uses the auxiliary **avoir**, the past participle agrees in gender (masculine or feminine) and number (singular or plural) **if** the direct object precedes (comes before) the verb in the sentence.

Look carefully at the following:

1.   Hier, j'ai acheté **des fleurs**
        I bought some flowers yesterday
        J'ai choisi **les fleurs** pour offrir à ma mère
        I chose the flowers for my mother
In these sentences, the word order is **Subject + verb+ <u>object</u>, in that order** so there is no change of spelling in the past participle because it follows the verb.

2.   **Les fleurs** que j'ai achet**ées** hier étaient très chères
        The flowers I bought yesterday were very expensive
        Je **les** ai choisi**es** pour offrir à ma mère
        *I chose **them** for my mother*
Here, in both sentences the **object comes before the verb**, so the past participle has to agree with the object.
In the clause - je **les** ai choisi**es** - notice that the object is a pronoun.

Perfect Tense with être (L'auxiliaire être)
There are 16 common verbs which form the perfect tense with **être** as the auxiliary. Most of them can be remembered in groups which are opposite (or nearly opposite) in meaning. These verbs and their compounds are marked with a *.

arriver*	descendre*	venir*	entrer*	naître*	tomber*
partir*	monter*	revenir*	rentrer*	mourir*	rester*
		aller*	sortir*		retourner*

When they are arranged in this order, the initial letters of the first verb in each group spell the word **ADVENT** - it might help in remembering them!

The important point with these verbs is that the past participle must agree with the subject:

     Example:

singular	masc	fem
je suis	venu	venue
tu es	venu	venue
vous êtes	venu	venue
il est	venu	
elle est		venue
on est	venu	
Chris est	venu (boy)	venue (girl)

plural	masc	fem
nous sommes	venus	venues
vous êtes	venus	venues
ils sont	venus	
elles sont		venues
les enfants sont	venus	

Vous can be masculine, feminine, singular or plural, so it has four past participle endings.

Following this rule, the past participle of **partir*** can be:
parti, partie, partis, parties
and the past participle of **sortir*** can be:
sorti, sortie, sortis, sorties

Similarly, the past participle of **descendre*** can be:
descendu, descendue, descendus, descendues

The past participle of **mourir*** can be:
mort, morte, morts, mortes

The past participles of the verbs from this group which end in -é
**arriver*, monter*, aller*, entrer*, rentrer*, naître*, tomber*,
rester*, retourner*** add an extra -**e, -s** or -**es** where needed:
allé, allée, allés, allées

Verbs used transitively (L'emploi transitif des verbes)
The verbs **descendre, monter, rentrer, sortir** can all be used with **avoir** if they have a direct object. The usual rules of agreement with **avoir** then apply.
Example: As-tu descendu les valises? Oui, je **les** ai descendu**es**
*Did you carry the cases down? Yes, I carried **them** down*
Est-ce qu'il a monté les bagages? Oui, il **les** a monté**s**
Has he carried the luggage upstairs? Yes, he carried it up
As-tu rentré le bois? L'as-tu rentré?
Did you bring in the wood? Did you bring it in?
A-t-il sorti la valise? Oui, il **l'**a sortie
Did he carry the case out? Yes, he carried it out

Compound Tenses with être - Reflexive Verbs
(L'auxiliaire être et les verbes pronominaux)
Reflexive verbs (also called pronominal verbs) are another group which take **être** as their auxiliary in forming their perfect tense. There are in fact several groups of these verbs.

In genuine reflexive verbs the subject performs the action to or for him/herself. There is agreement of the past participle because the reflexive pronoun is the direct object of the verb. It follows the preceding direct object rule which affects avoir verbs (see page 60)

Example: Elle s'est lavée *She washed (herself)*

Here the **se** is the **direct** object and comes before the verb, thus requiring agreement.

However, the reflexive pronoun is not always the **direct** object of the verb:

Example: Elle s'est coupé le doigt
She cut her finger
Elle s'est brossé les cheveux
She brushed her hair

In these examples, the reflexive pronoun is the **indirect** object; the **direct** object of the verb is the noun and it is following the verb, so no agreement is necessary.

In reciprocal pronominal verbs where the subjects perform the action of the verb to/for each other, the same principle applies. Where the pronoun is the **direct** object, agreement is shown.

    Example: Paul et Michelle se sont **vus** hier
                        Paul and Michelle saw each other yesterday

Where the pronoun is the **indirect** object there is no agreement.

    Example: Paul et Michelle ne se sont jamais parlé
                        Paul and Michelle have never spoken to each other

Formation of the perfect tense of reflexive verbs
(La formation du passé composé des verbes pronominaux)
The Perfect tense of a reflexive verb is formed by the auxiliary **être** and the past participle.

Se réveiller* - *to wake up*	Masculine	Feminine
je me suis	réveillé	réveillée
tu t'es	réveillé	réveillée
il s'est	réveillé	
elle s'est		réveillée
Chris s'est	réveillé	réveillée
on s'est	réveillé	
nous nous sommes	réveillé**s**	réveillé**es**
vous vous êtes	réveillé(**s**)	réveillée(**s**)
ils se sont	réveillé**s**	
elles se sont		réveillé**es**
les enfants se sont	réveillé**s**	

Vous endings depend on whether vous is masculine, feminine, singular or plural. Where an irregular past participle - **assis** - ends in **-s** no further **s** is required for the masculine plural agreement - ils se sont assis

The Perfect Infinitive (L'infinitif passé)
A perfect infinitive is used after **après** to express the idea of having done something. In English we say *after ...ing*.

    Example: *After eating his tea, he went out*

but in French use après + avoir (or après + être) + the past participle. The the usual rules of agreement for verbs taking être in the perfect tense apply.

    Example: Après avoir mangé, il est sorti
                        After eating he went out
                        Après être arrivé**e** à l'école, **elle** a cherché ses copines
                        After arriving at school, she went to look for her friends
                        Après s'être habillé**s**, **ils** sont descendus
                        After getting dressed, they went downstairs

The Imperfect Tense (L'Imparfait)

Use of the imperfect tense (L'emploi de l'imparfait)
This is the tense which translates the English *was -ing*, or *used to*.
It is a tense with several distinct tasks.

1. It is used for describing events, people or feelings in the past.
    Example: Il faisait noir, il neigeait et le petit garçon avait peur
               It was dark, it was snowing and the little boy was afraid

2. It is used for talking or writing about repeated actions in the past.
    Example: Chaque matin il quittait la maison à huit heures
               He left the house at eight o'clock every morning

3. It is used for talking or writing about incomplete actions in the past - actions interrupted by another action.
    Example: Comme je marchais le long de la rue
               As I was walking down the road

4. It is used in reported speech.
    Example: "Je suis très malheureuse", a-t-elle dit (direct speech)
               "I am very unhappy", she said
    becomes   Elle a dit qu'elle était très malheureuse (reported speech)
               She said that she was very unhappy

Formation of the imperfect tense (La formation de l'imparfait)
To form the imperfect tense of a verb, regular or irregular, you need to know the **nous** form of the present tense.

1. Remove the **-ons** ending from the **nous** form.
    So: nous allons becomes   **all-**
          nous finissons becomes   **finiss-**
          nous disons becomes   **dis-**

2. To these stems add the endings for the imperfect tense:
    -ais, -ais, -ait, -ions, -iez, -aient

Travailler - *to work*

je travaill**ais**	*I was working, I used to work, I worked*
tu travaill**ais**	*you were working, you used to work, you worked*
il travaill**ait**	*he was working, he used to work, he worked*
elle travaill**ait**	*she was working, she used to work, she worked*
on travaill**ait**	*one was working, one used to work, one worked*
Chris travaill**ait**	*Chris was working, used to work, worked*
nous travaill**ions**	*we were working, we used to work, we worked*
vous travaill**iez**	*you were working, you used to work, you worked*
ils travaill**aient**	*they were working, they used to work, they worked*
elles travaill**aient**	*they were working, they used to work, they worked*
les enfants travaill**aient**	*the children were working, used to work, worked*

Verbs   *French Grammar*

Finir - *to finish*

je finiss**ais**	*I was finishing, I did finish, I finished*
tu finiss**ais**	*you were finishing, you did finish, you finished,*
il finiss**ait**	*he was finishing, he did finish, he finished*
elle finiss**ait**	*she was finishing, she did finish, she finished*
on finiss**ait**	*one was finishing, one did finish, one finished*
Chris finiss**ait**	*Chris was finishing, did finish, finished*
nous finiss**ions**	*we were finishing, we did finish, we finished*
vous finiss**iez**	*you were finishing, you did finish, you finished*
ils finiss**aient**	*they were finishing, they did finish, they finished*
elles finiss**aient**	*they were finishing, they did finish, they finished*
les enfants finiss**aient**	*the children were finishing, did finish, finished*

Répondre - *to answer*

je répond**ais**	*I was answering, I did answer, I answered*
tu répond**ais**	*you were answering, you did answer, you answere*
il répond**ait**	*he was answering, he did answer, he answered*
elle répond**ait**	*she was answering, she did answer, she answered*
on répond**ait**	*one was answering, one did answer, one answered*
Chris répond**ait**	*Chris was answering, did answer, answered*
nous répond**ions**	*we were answering, we did answer, we answered*
vous répond**iez**	*you were answering, you did answer, you answered*
ils répond**aient**	*they were answering, they did answer, answered*
elles répond**aient**	*they were answering, they did answer, answered*
les enfants répond**aient**	*the children were answering, did answer, answered*

3. **être** is the only irregular verb in this tense and it is irregular only in the form of its stem **ét**.

   Once this is established, the endings are added in the normal way.

j'ét**ais**	*I was, I used to be*
tu ét**ais**	*you were, you used to be*
il ét**ait**	*he was, he used to be*
elle ét**ait**	*she was, she used to be*
on ét**ait**	*one was, one used to be*
Chris ét**ait**	*Chris was, Chris used to be*
nous ét**ions**	*we were, we used to be*
vous ét**iez**	*you were, you used to be*
ils ét**aient**	*they were, they used to be*
elles ét**aient**	*they were, they used to be*
les enfants ét**aient**	*the children were, the children used to be*

French Grammar *Verbs*

4. The **-er** verbs which have an extra **e** in the **nous** form of the present tense to soften the **-g** do not need this **-e** in the **nous** and **vous** of the imperfect tense because of the **-i** in the ending.

>   je voyageais   nous voyag**ions**
>   tu voyageais   vous voyag**iez**
>   il voyageait   ils voyageaient
>   elle voyageait   elles voyageaient
>   on voyageait   les enfants voyageaient
>   Chris voyageait

   Other verbs of this type are:
   changer, échanger, loger, manger, nager, obliger, partager, ranger.

5. The **-er** verbs which have **ç** in the **nous** form of the present tense to soften the **-c** do not need this **-ç** in the **nous** and **vous** of the imperfect tense because of the **-i** in the ending.

>   je commençais   nous commen**cions**
>   tu commençais   vous commen**ciez**
>   il commençait   ils commençaient
>   elle commençait   elles commençaient
>   on commençait   les enfants commençaient
>   Chris commençait

   Other verbs of this type are:
   avancer, lancer, menacer, placer, prononcer, remplacer

THE PLUPERFECT TENSE (LE PLUS-QUE-PARFAIT)

Use of the pluperfect tense (L'emploi du plus-que-parfait)

This tense translates the English
   had given   *had* been thinking   *had* played

1. The pluperfect tense is used to talk or write about events in the past which had happened before other past events took place.

   Example: Ils avaient acheté une voiture neuve deux jours avant leur départ
   They had bought a new car two days before they left

2. It is also used to report what other people had said (reported speech).

   Example: "Je suis arrivé au collège à neuf heures" (direct speech)
              "I got to school at nine o'clock"
   becomes   Il a dit qu'il était arrivé au collège à neuf heures (reported speech)
              He said that he got to school at nine o'clock

Verbs   *French Grammar*

Formation of the pluperfect tense (La formation du plus-que-parfait)

The pluperfect tense is formed in the same way as the perfect tense, except that the imperfect tense of the auxiliary **avoir** or **être** is used in place of the present tense.
All the rules concerning agreement of the past participle apply in exactly the same way.

avoir verbs	**être** verbs	**reflexive** verbs
j'avais vu	j'étais allé(e)	je m'étais levé(e)
tu avais vu	tu étais allé(e)	tu t'étais levé(e)
il avait vu	il était allé	il s'était levé
elle avait vu	elle était allée	elle s'était levée
on avait vu	on était allé	on s'était levé
Chris avait vu	Chris était allé(e)	Chris s'était levé(e)
nous avions vu	nous étions allé(e)s	nous nous étions levé(e)s
vous aviez vu	vous étiez allé(e)(s)	vous vous étiez levé(e)(s)
ils avaient vu	ils étaient allés	ils s'étaient levés
elles avaient vu	elles étaient allées	elles s'étaient levées
les enfants avaient vu	les enfants étaient allés	les enfants s'étaient levés

THE PRESENT PARTICIPLE (LE PARTICIPE PRÉSENT)

Use of the present participle (L'emploi du participe présent)

Each verb has a present participle as well as a past participle.
The present participle in English ends in **-ing**
         work**ing**, finish**ing**, answer**ing**, etc.
In French the present participle ends in **-ant**
         travaill**ant**, finiss**ant**, répond**ant**, etc.

1.   When used as a verb the present participle does not have to change its spelling.

         Example: **Voyant** qu'il dormait, elle sortit
                       Seeing that he was asleep, she went out
                       Ils sont sortis, la **laissant** seule à la maison
                       They went out, leaving her alone in the house

but when used as an adjective the present participle has to agree with its noun.

         Example: une femme **souriante** - *a smiling woman*
                       des enfants **désobéissants** - *disobedient children*

2.   **en + present participle** is used to describe two actions which are being performed by one person at approximately the same time.

         Example: Il s'est foulé la cheville **en jouant** au rugby
                       He sprained his ankle playing rugby
                       "Bonjour," a-t-il dit **en souriant**
                       "Good Morning," he said with a smile

French Grammar *Verbs*

3. *On, while, by, when* doing something are all translated by **en** + present participle.

> Example: **En arrivant** chez moi, j'ai ouvert la porte
> *On arriving home I opened the door*
> Il a cassé la fenêtre **en jouant** dans le jardin
> *He broke the window **while** playing in the garden*
> **En travaillant** dur, vous réussirez
> ***By** working hard, you will succeed*
> **En** me **voyant**, il est parti à la hâte
> ***When** he saw me, he left in a hurry*

4. **Tout** can be put with **en** to give the idea of two actions taking place simultaneously.

> Example **Tout en parlant**, elle préparait le repas
> *While she was talking she was preparing the meal*

5. **En** and the present participle are used to show method of motion after verbs such as **entrer*, sortir*, descendre*, monter*, traverser**.

> Example: Elle est entrée **en boitant**
> *She came in **limping***
> Il est sorti **en courant**
> *He **ran** outside*

6. Where we would use a present participle in English, it is often better to use a relative clause in French.

> Example: Je les voyais **qui s'approchaient** de la maison
> *I saw them **coming** towards the house*
> Il y avait une vingtaine d'enfants **qui jouaient** dans la forêt
> *There were about 20 children **playing** in the forest*

Formation of the present participle (La formation du participe présent)
To form the present participle, take the **nous** form of the present tense, remove the **-ons** ending and add **-ant**.

> Example: **-er** verbs - travaill**ons** - becomes travaill**ant**
> **-ir** verbs - finiss**ons** - becomes finiss**ant**
> **-re** verbs - répond**ons** - becomes répond**ant**

Remember that there are three exceptions: **avoir, être** and **savoir**:

> avoir   has the present participle   **ayant**
> être   has the present participle   **étant**
> savoir   has the present participle   **sachant**

The Future Tense (Le Futur)

Use of the future tense (L'emploi du futur)
The future tense in French is used:
- to talk and write about things which definitely **will** happen
- to refer to events which will take place at some time in the future rather than in the short term.

There are more forms of the future in English than there are in French.

    Example: *He will see her* and *He will be seeing her*
                      will both be translated as **Il la verra**

For speakers of English there can be problems with what seem at first to be "hidden" future tenses after **quand**.

    Example: Il la verra quand il viendra
                      (both verbs in the future)
                      *He will see her **when he comes***
                      (one verb in the future, one in the present)

Remember to use the future tense of the verbs in both parts of the sentence in French, with time words such as **quand**, **lorsque** *(when)* **aussitôt que** *(as soon as)*.

    Example: Quand je la **verrai** je lui **donnerai** la lettre
                      *When I **see** her I**'ll give** her the letter*
                      Elle t'**écrira** quand elle **sera** à Paris
                      *She **will write** to you when she **is** in Paris*

Use future tense for future time!

Use of the immediate future (L'emploi du futur proche)
If you wish to talk or write about something which will happen in the fairly near future, there is also the option of using a construction which is similar to the idea of the English.

In French, in order to say *He is going to play football next Saturday*, use the present tense of **aller + the infinitive of the verb**.

    Example: Il **va jouer** au football samedi prochain
                      He is going to play football next Saturday
                      He is playing football next Saturday
                      He will be playing football next Saturday
                      Je **vais lire** un journal
                      I am going to read a newspaper
                      I shall read a newspaper
                      Tu **vas partir** bientôt
                      You are going to leave soon
                      You will be leaving soon
                      Ils **vont arriver** tard
                      They will be arriving late
                      They are going to arrive late

French Grammar *Verbs*

Formation of the future tense (La formation du futur)
To form the future tense of regular **-er** and **-ir** verbs, you add the endings:
  -ai, -as, -a, -ons, -ez, -ont to the infinitive.
To form the future tense of an **-re** verb you have to remove the final **-e** from the infinitive before adding the endings.

Travailler - *to work*

je travaill**erai**	*I will work, I will be working*
tu travaill**eras**	*you will work, you will be working*
il travaill**era**	*he will work, he will be working*
elle travaill**era**	*she will work, she will be working*
on travaill**era**	*one will work, one will be working*
Chris travaill**era**	*Chris will work, will be working*
nous travaill**erons**	*we will work, we will be working*
vous travaill**erez**	*you will work, you will be working*
ils travaill**eront**	*they will work, they will be working*
elles travaill**eront**	*they will work, they will be working*
les enfants travaill**eront**	*the children will work, will be working*

Finir - *to finish*

je finir**ai**	*I will finish, I will be finishing*
tu finir**as**	*you will finish, you will be finishing*
il finir**a**	*he will finish, he will be finishing*
elle finir**a**	*she will finish, she will be finishing*
on finir**a**	*one will finish, one will be finishing*
Chris finir**a**	*Chris will finish, will be finishing*
nous finir**ons**	*we will finish, we will be finishing*
vous finir**ez**	*you will finish, you will be finishing*
ils finir**ont**	*they will finish, they will be finishing*
elles finir**ont**	*they will finish, they will be finishing*
les enfants finir**ont**	*the children will finish, will be finishing*

Répondre - *to answer*

je répondr**ai**	*I will answer, I will be answering*
tu répondr**as**	*you will answer, you will be answering*
il répondr**a**	*he will answer, he will be answering*
elle répondr**a**	*she will answer, she will be answering*
on répondr**a**	*one will answer, one will be answering*
Chris répondr**a**	*Chris will answer, will be answering*
nous répondr**ons**	*we will answer, we will be answering*
vous répondr**ez**	*you will answer, you will be answering*
ils répondr**ont**	*they will answer, they will be answering*
elles répondr**ont**	*they will answer, they will be answering*
les enfants répondr**ont**	*the children will answer, will be answering*

Irregular future tenses (Des verbes irreguliers au futur)
There are some commonly used verbs which have an irregular stem in the future and these have to be learned individually.
Once you know the stem, you can add the endings in the normal way.

infinitive	future	infinitive	future
acheter	j'achèterai	falloir	il faudra
aller*	j'irai	jeter	je jetterai
appeler	j'appellerai	mourir*	je mourrai
s'asseoir*	je m'assiérai	pleuvoir	il pleuvra
avoir	j'aurai	pouvoir	je pourrai
courir	je courrai	recevoir	je recevrai
devoir	je devrai	savoir	je saurai
envoyer	j'enverrai	tenir	je tiendrai
être	je serai	venir*	je viendrai
faire	je ferai	voir	je verrai

THE CONDITIONAL TENSE (LE CONDITIONNEL)

Use of the conditional tense (L'emploi du conditionnel)
This is the tense used to talk or write about things which you **would** do - if ...
It is how you express the idea of conditions.

>   Example: *If I were rich,* ***I would travel*** *round the world*
>   Si j'étais riche, **je ferais** le tour du monde

Notice that the pattern of tenses you use with **si** follows a similar pattern to the tenses we use in English:

>   *If it rains, we'll go to the museum*
>   S'il pleut, nous **irons** au musée   (present + future)
>   *If it were to rain, we would go to the museum*
>   S'il pleuvait, nous **irions** au musée   (imperfect + conditional)
>   *If I had known, I would have told you*
>   Si je l'avais su, je te l'**aurais** dit   (pluperfect + conditional perfect)

Formation of the conditional tense (La formation du conditionnel)
The conditional tense is something of a "mongrel" in its formation! It is a future tense crossed with the imperfect - you combine the stem of the future tense with the endings of the imperfect tense! The imperfect endings are **-ais, -ais, -ait, -ions, -iez, -aient**.

infinitive	conditional	infinitive	conditional
-er verbs	je travaille**rais**	être	je se**rais**
	j'aime**rais**	faire	je fe**rais**
-ir verbs	je fini**rais**	pouvoir	je pour**rais**
-re verbs	je répond**rais**	savoir	je sau**rais**
aller*	j'i**rais**	venir*	je viend**rais**
avoir	j'au**rais**	vouloir	je voud**rais**
devoir	je dev**rais**	voir	je ver**rais**

French Grammar *Verbs*

THE PAST HISTORIC (LE PASSÉ SIMPLE)

Use of the past historic tense (L'emploi du passé simple)
This is the tense used in the narrative sections of stories and novels, in history books and in some parts of newspapers to describe.
- a completed action in the past
- a series of completed events in a story
- an action in the past which happened on one occasion only

 Example: Elle monta au troisième étage   *She went up to the third floor*
 Il mourut en 1930   *He died in 1930*
 Il sortit de la maison, traversa la rue et entra dans le magasin
 He left the house, crossed the street and went into the shop

Remember that the past historic is **never** used in letters and e-mails or in conversation.

Formation of the past historic tense (La formation du passé simple)
To form the past historic of any regular **-er** verb and **aller,** you take off the final **-er** of the infinitive and add the endings:
 -ai, -as, -a, -âmes, -âtes, -èrent

Travailler - *to work*

 je travaill**ai**   *I worked*
 tu travaill**as**   *you worked*
 il travaill**a**   *he worked*
 elle travaill**a**   *she worked*
 on travaill**a**   *one worked*
 Chris travaill**a**   *Chris worked*
 nous travaill**âmes**   *we worked*
 vous travaill**âtes**   *you worked*
 ils travaill**èrent**   *they worked*
 elles travaill**èrent**   *they worked*
 les enfants travaill**èrent**   *the children worked*

To form the past historic of a regular **-ir** and **-re** verb, you take off the final **-ir** and **-re** of the infinitive and add the endings:
 -is, -is, -it, -îmes, -îtes, -irent

Finir - *to finish*

 je fin**is**   *I finished*
 tu fin**is**   *you finished*
 il fin**it**   *he finished*
 elle fin**it**   *she finished*
 Chris fin**it**   *Chris finished*
 nous fin**îmes**   *we finished*
 vous fin**îtes**   *you finished*
 ils fin**irent**   *they finished*
 elles fin**irent**   *they finished*
 les enfants fin**irent**   *the children finished*

Répondre - *to answer*

je répond**is**	*I answered*
tu répond**is**	*you answered*
il répond**it**	*he answered*
elle répond**it**	*she answered*
on répond**it**	*one answered*
Chris répond**it**	*Chris answered*
nous répond**îmes**	*we answered*
vous répond**îtes**	*you answered*
ils répond**irent**	*they answered*
elles répond**irent**	*they answered*
les enfants répond**irent**	*the children answered*

Irregular verbs in the past historic

Common irregular verbs tend to follow one of two patterns in the past historic
They follow the **-is** pattern, (like **répondre**), with the endings **-is, -is, -it, -îmes, -îtes, -irent**
or the **–us** pattern (like **vouloir**), with the endings **-us, -us, ut, ûmes, ûtes, urent**

Example of -is pattern:

Comprendre - *to understand*

je comp**ris**	*I understood*
tu comp**ris**	*you understood*
il comp**rit**	*he understood*
elle comp**rit**	*she understood*
on comp**rit**	*one understood*
Chris comp**rit**	*Chris understood*
nous comp**rîmes**	*we understood*
vous comp**rîtes**	*you understood*
ils comp**rirent**	*they understood*
les enfants comp**rirent**	*the children understood*

Irregular verbs which follow the **-is** pattern include:

Infinitive	**Past Historic**	**Infinitive**	**Past Historic**
apprendre	il apprit	poursuivre	il poursuivit
s'asseoir*	il s'assit	prendre	il prit
couvrir	il couvrit	promettre	il promit
dire	il dit	rire	il rit
dormir	il dormit	sentir	il sentit
faire	il fit	servir	il servit
mettre	il mit	sortir*	il sortit
offrir	il offrit	sourire	il sourit
ouvrir	il ouvrit	suivre	il suivit
partir*	il partit	surprendre	il surprit
permettre	il permit	voir	il vit

Example of -us pattern:

Vouloir - *to wish, to want*

je voul**us**	*I wished, I wanted*
tu voul**us**	*you wished, you wanted*
il voul**ut**	*he wished, he wanted*
elle voul**ut**	*she wished, she wanted*
on voul**ut**	*one wished, one wanted*
Chris voul**ut**	*Chris wished, wanted*
nous voul**ûmes**	*we wished, we wanted*
vous voul**ûtes**	*you wished, you wanted*
ils voul**urent**	*they wished, they wanted*
les enfants voul**urent**	*the children wished, wanted*

Irregular verbs which follow the **-us** pattern include:

Infinitive	Past Historic	Infinitive	Past Historic
apercevoir	il aperçut	falloir	il fallut
avoir	il eut	lire	il lut
boire	il but	paraître	il parut
connaître	il connut	pleuvoir	il plut
courir	il courut	pouvoir	il put
croire	il crut	savoir	il sut
devoir	il dut	se taire*	il se tut
être	il fut	vivre	il vécut

Other patterns for irregular verbs in the past historic

1. **conduire, construire** and **écrire** add an extra syllable before the **-is** pattern endings

conduire	il condu**is**it
construire	il constru**is**it
écrire	il écr**iv**it

2. **devenir***, **revenir***, **se souvenir*** (**de**) and **venir*** follow this pattern:

je vins	nous vînmes
tu vins	vous vîntes
il vint	ils vinrent

3. **contenir, obtenir, retenir** and **tenir** follow this pattern:

je tins	nous tînmes
tu tins	vous tîntes
il tint	ils tinrent

The Passive Voice (La Voix Passive)

Use of the passive voice (L'emploi de la voix passive)

Contrast *We follow the children*
         Nous suivons les enfants   (active voice)
with   *We are being followed by the children*
         Nous sommes suivis par les enfants   (passive voice)

Formation of the passive (La formation de la voix passive)

To form the passive you use **être** + the past participle of the verb to be made passive. This past participle **must** agree with the subject of the sentence.

> Example: "J'ai été piquée par un moustique!" a dit Marie-Laure
> *"I've been bitten by a mosquito!" said Marie-Laure*

All tenses of the passive can be made up by using the appropriate tense of **être** + the past participle of the verb to be made passive:

> Example: present: elle est trouvée   *she is found*
>   future: elle sera trouvée   *she will be found*
>   imperfect: ils étaient trouvés   *they were found*
>   perfect: elles ont été trouvées   *they (f) were, have been found*

The past participle agrees in gender and number with the subject.

Avoidance of the passive (Comment éviter d'utiliser la voix passive)

The passive is avoided as far as possible by using one of the following alternatives:

1. By using **on**.

   > Example: On l'a trouvé près de la gare *He was found near the station*

2. By using a reflexive verb.

   > Example: Je m'étonne que ...   *I am surprised that ...*
   >   Cela ne se fait pas   *That is not done*

3. By turning the sentence round, and thus making the verb active.

   > Example: Il a été mordu par un chien   *He was bitten by a dog*
   >   becomes Le chien l'a mordu   *The dog bit him*

4. By using an impersonal verb.

   > Example: Il est interdit de fumer   *Smoking is not allowed/No smoking*

French Grammar *Verbs*

IMPERATIVE FORMS (L'IMPÉRATIF)

Use of the imperative (L'emploi de l'impératif)
Imperative forms, also called command forms, are used to tell someone to do something, or not to do something. There are three imperative forms for each verb.
In most cases they are derived from the **tu**, **nous** and **vous** forms of the verb.
Remember that you should select the **tu** and **vous** forms according to the usual rules for **tu** and **vous** (see page 41).

Formation of the imperative (La formation de l'impératif)

For **-ir** and **-re** verbs, you omit the **tu**, **nous** or **vous** and just use the one word.

Example: **Finis** ton travail! **Réponds** à la question!
Finissons le travail ensemble! **Répondons** à la question
Finissez votre travail **Répondez** à la question!

For **-er verbs** (and in this instance, **aller** behaves like an **-er** verb) there is one difference. You omit the final **-s** of the **tu** form of the verb.

Example: **Regarde** le livre! **Va** à la porte!
Regardons le livre! **Allons** à la porte!
Regardez le livre! **Allez** à la porte!

There is a special form of the imperative of **aller**.
Vas-y!   *Get on with it!*   *Go on!*

To form the imperative of a reflexive verb you add a version of the reflexive pronoun to the verb with a hyphen.

Example: Assieds-**toi**!   Asseyons-**nous**!   Asseyez-**vous**!

To form a negative imperative **ne** (or **n'**) and **pas** are put around the verb.

Example: **Ne** finis **pas** ton travail! **Ne** réponds **pas** à la question!
Ne finissons **pas** notre travail! **Ne** répondons **pas**!
Ne finissez **pas** votre travail **Ne** répondez **pas**!

With reflexive verbs, add the **ne** (or **n'**) and **pas** and move the pronoun.

Example: **Ne** te fâche **pas**!   **Ne** nous fâchons **pas**!   **Ne** vous fâchez **pas**!

Irregular imperative forms
Four of the common verbs have irregular imperative forms.

avoir	être	savoir	vouloir
aie	sois	sache	veuille
ayons	soyons	sachons	veuillons
ayez	soyez	sachez	veuillez

Verbs   *French Grammar*

NEGATIVES (LES NÉGATIONS)

Use of negatives (L'emploi des négations)

Negatives are words put with a verb to change its meaning; it then says that something *will not/will never/will no longer* happen.

In French, negatives usually have two parts - **ne** (or **n'**) and another word which varies according to meaning.

ne ... pas	*not*	ne ... ni ... ni	*neither ... nor*
ne ... jamais	*never*	ne ... aucun(e)	*no, not one*
ne ... rien	*nothing*	ne ... nulle part	*nowhere*
ne ... personne	*nobody*	ne ... pas du tout	*definitely not*
ne ... plus	*no longer*	ne ... point	<u>not</u> *(rarely used)*
ne ... que	*only*	ne ... guère	*hardly*

Word order with negatives (L'ordre des mots)

1. The general rule is that in simple tenses the **ne** comes before the verb and the **pas/plus**, etc follow it.

    Example: Je **ne** regarde **pas** la télévision   *I don't watch television*
                      Je **ne** regarde **jamais** la télévision   *I never watch television*
                      Je **ne** regarde **plus** la télévision   *I don't watch television any more*

2. When you use a negative with a compound tense the position of the second part of the negative varies. With the negatives listed here, the second part of the negative comes before the past participle:

    Example: Je **n'**ai **pas** vu le film   *I did not see the film*
                      Je **n'**ai **jamais** visité la France   *I have never been to France*
                      Je **n'**ai **rien** mangé hier   *I did not eat anything yesterday*
                      Je **n'**y ai **plus** pensé   *I did not think about it any more*
                      Il **n'**a **pas du tout** compris   *He did not understand at all*

    With the negatives listed here, the second part follows the past participle:

    Example: Je **n'**ai vu **personne**   *I didn't see anyone*
                      Il **n'**a eu **aucune** idée   *He had no idea*
                      Elle **n'**a eu **aucun** problème   *She had no problem*
                      Il **n'**a eu **ni** ami **ni** ennemi   *He had neither friend nor enemy*
                      Je **ne** l'ai vu **nulle part**   *I didn't see him anywhere*
                      Je **n'**ai vu **que** son frère et lui   *I only saw him and his brother*

3. When you make a reflexive verb negative, the reflexive pronoun follows the **ne**.

    Example: Je ne **me** réveille pas tôt   *I don't wake up early*
                      Il ne **s'**est pas couché tard   *He didn't go to bed late*

French Grammar *Verbs*

4. If there are other pronouns before the verb they also follow the **ne**.

   Example: Elle ne **me le** donne pas   *She does not give it to me*
             Il n'**y** est pas allé   *He did not go there*
             Vous ne **m'en** avez pas donné   *You did not give me any (of it)*
             Il n'**y en** a pas   *There isn't any*

5. Negatives are usually followed by **de** or **d'** just as the word *any* follows negatives in English.

   Example: Je n'ai pas **de** pain   *I haven't got any bread*
             Je n'ai plus **d'**argent   *I haven't got any more money*

6. Note the word order when the negative is either the subject or the first word of the sentence.

   Example: **Personne n'**est venu
             Nobody came
             Rien ne bouge
             Nothing moves
             Jamais je **n'**oublierai ce que tu as dit
             I'll never forget what you said
             Aucune voiture **n'**attendait à la gare
             There was no car waiting at the station
             Ni mon père **ni** ma mère **ne** viendront
             Neither my father nor my mother will be coming

7. You can use two negatives in one sentence.

   Example: Il **ne** fait **plus rien**   *He no longer does anything*
             Je **ne** la reverrai **jamais plus**   *I shall never ever see her again*
             On **n'**y voit **jamais personne**   *You never see anyone there*

8. If you want to make the infinitive of a verb negative, you place **both parts before** the infinitive.

   Example: Je leur ai dit de **ne pas** attendre
             I told them not to wait
             Il a choisi de **ne rien** dire
             He has chosen to say nothing
             Elle a décidé de **ne jamais** retourner à Marseille
             She decided never to go back to Marseilles

9. With **ne ... personne, ne ... que,** the two parts are separated by the infinitive.

   Example: J'ai l'intention de **ne** voir **personne** demain
             I don't intend to see anyone tomorrow
             Il s'étonnait de **ne** trouver **qu'**un livre
             He was surprised to find only one book

10. **Jamais, personne** and **rien** are used as one word negative answers to questions.

> Example: Qu'est-ce que tu as acheté au marché? **Rien**!
> *What did you buy at the market? Nothing!*
> Qui as-tu vu? **Personne!**
> *Whom did you see? Nobody!*
> Est-ce que tu fais du ski? **Jamais!**
> *Do you go skiing? Never!*

11. **Non** and **pas** are also words used to give answers in the negative.
Non *(no)* can be made less brusque by the addition of words such as Monsieur, Madame, Mademoiselle.

> Example: Non, Madame   Non, Monsieur

Notice also **Je crois que non** - *I don't think so, I think not*

Pas is often found in phrases such as:
> **Pas** par là! - *Not that way!*
> **Pas** moi! - *Not me!*

12. When using **ne ... que** you must place the **que** immediately before the word or phrase to which the idea of *only* applies.

> Example: Il **ne** voit sa mère **que** le mardi
> *He sees his mother only on Tuesdays*
> Elle **ne** fait des photos **que** pendant les vacances
> *She takes photos only in the holidays*

13. In everyday speech the **ne** is often omitted, or slurred over. This may **not** be done when writing.

"C'est pas vrai!" must be written as: "Ce **n'**est pas vrai!"
"Je sais pas!" must be written as: "Je **ne** sais pas!"

QUESTION FORMS (LES QUESTIONS)

Formation of questions (Comment poser les questions?)
These are also known as interrogatives.
There are five ways in which you can ask questions in French.

1. In speaking, a rising tone of voice can turn a statement into a question.

    Example: Vous aimez le fromage?   *Do you like cheese?*

2. By putting **n'est-ce pas** at the end of a sentence.

    Example: Il fait froid, **n'est-ce pas?**   *Isn't it cold?*
    It's cold, isn't it?

3. By writing or saying **est-ce que** or **est-ce qu'** at the beginning of the sentence.

    Example: **Est-ce que** vous aimez le fromage?   *Do you like cheese?*

4. By inverting the subject and verb. (Attach the subject to the verb with a hyphen)

    Example: Aimes-tu le fromage?   *Do you like cheese?*

    However, if you use a verb with a vowel as its ending, put in an extra **-t-**.

    Example: Paul, joue-**t**-il au football?   *Does Paul play football?*
    Ta mère, va-t-elle souvent au théâtre?
    Does your mother often go to the theatre?

5. By using question words at the beginning of the sentence.

    Example: Où vas-tu passer les vacances de Pâques?
    Where are you going to spend the Easter holidays?

Some common question words

Combien? (de)	*How much? How many?*
Comment?	*How? What?*
Comment est ...?	*What is ... like?*
D'où?	*Where from?*
Où?	*Where? Where ... to?*
Pourquoi?	*Why?*
Quand?	*When?*
Que?	*What*
Quel/Quelle/Quels/Quelles?	*Which?* (adjectives – they agree with the noun)
Qu'est-ce que?	*What?*
Qu'est-ce qui?	*What?*
Qui?	*Who?*
Qui est-ce qui?	*Who?*
Quoi?	*What?*

Verbs   *French Grammar*

MODAL VERBS (VERBES AUXILIAIRES MODAUX)

Use of modal verbs (L'emploi des verbes auxiliaires modaux)
There are several verbs in French including **devoir, pouvoir, savoir** and **vouloir** which need special attention.
They usually need another verb to follow them, and they can have special meanings in certain tenses.
They are also all irregular, and they all appear in the Verb Table (pages 88-106).

Devoir – *to owe, to have to*

This verb has two meanings - *to owe, to have to*.
When it is used in its meaning of *to owe* it functions on its own, without another verb.

        Example: Il me **doit** 30 euros   *He owes me 30 euros*
                          Je vous **dois** combien?   *How much do I owe you?*

When devoir means *to have to*, it must have another verb to follow it in the sentence, and that verb is always in the **infinitive**.

        Example: Je dois **partir**   *I have to leave, I must leave*
                          Je devrai **partir**   *I will/I shall have to go*

There are various shades of meaning for **devoir**.

1.   **must** in the sense of **being obliged to**

        Example: Nous devons aller au collège   *We **have to** go to school*

2.   **must** in the sense of **something being arranged, being supposed to**

        Example: Je dois aller voir mes cousins
                          I am supposed to/I have to visit my cousins

3.   In the perfect tense it can mean either **(have) had to** or **must have**.

        Example: Nous avons dû aller voir des amis hier
                          *We **had to** go and see some friends yesterday*
                          J'ai dû laisser les clés à la maison!
                          *I **must have** left the keys at home!*

4.   In the conditional tense it can mean **should** or **ought to**.

        Example: Je devrais lui écrire
                          *I **ought to**/I (really) **should** write to him/her*

French Grammar　　　　　　　　　　　　　　　　　　　　　　　　　　*Verbs*

Pouvoir – *to be able to*

Pouvoir must always be used with a second verb following it and this second verb is always in the **infinitive**.

    Example: Nous pouvons **partir** à 10 heures
                    We can leave at 10 o'clock

There are various shades of meaning for **pouvoir**.

1. It has the meaning of **can** in the sense of **may** or **having permission to**.

    Example: Tu peux venir la voir demain   *You **can** come and see her tomorrow*
                  Puis-je vous aider?   ***May** I help you?*

2. It has the meaning of **can** in the sense of **being able to**.

    Example: Elle ne peut pas courir très vite   *She **can't** run very fast*

3. It has the meaning of **may** in the sense of **it is possible**.

    Example: Il peut arriver ce soir   *He **may** come this evening*

Savoir – *to know, to know how to*

1.   **Savoir** can be used on its own, without a second verb and means *to know*.

    Example: Je **sais** son nom et son adresse   *I know his/her name and address*
                  Comment le **savez**-vous?   *How do you know that?*
                  Savez-vous s'il vient?   *Do you know whether he is coming?*

2.   It can also mean *to realise*.

    Example: **Sais-tu** ce que tu fais?   *Do you realise what you are doing?*

3.   It can be used with a second verb to mean **to know how to**.

    Example: Je **sais** nager   *I can, **I know how to** swim*

If you have to convey the idea of *to know*, it is worth remembering that the verb **connaître** also means *to know*.
The difference between the two is that **savoir** conveys the idea of *to have knowledge of* science, a language, geography, etc, whereas **connaître** conveys the idea of *being acquainted with* a person, a town, a country, a book, a film.

    Example: Je **sais** où se trouve la Tour Eiffel, mais je ne la **connais** pas
                  I know where the Eiffel Tower is, but I do not know it
                  (= I have not been there)

Vouloir – *to want, to wish*

Vouloir is always used with a second verb following, and that verb is always in the infinitive.

Example: Nous **voulons** le voir   *We want to see it*
           Elle ne **voulait** pas aller   *She did not want to/was not willing to go*
           Voulez-vous signer, s'il vous plaît   *Sign, please*
           Je voudrais le voir, s'il vous plaît   *I would like to see it, please*

Je voudrais is also used as a polite way of saying *I want*.

Example: Je **voudrais** une glace   *I would like/I want an ice-cream*

Je voudrais can also mean *I wish*.

Example: **Je voudrais** savoir son nom   *I wish I knew his name*

Note: **Que veut dire ...?**   *What does ... mean?*

THE INFINITIVE (L'INFINITIF)

In addition to modal verbs, there are many other circumstances in which a second verb (in the infinitive) is required.
The infinitive may either be placed straight after the first verb, or it may require **à** or **de**.
Unfortunately, there is no easy way of knowing which method is used.
You just have to learn the verbs and their individual requirements!

Verbs followed by the infinitive (Les verbes suivis directement de l'infinitif)

Some common verbs are followed directly by an infinitive and need no preposition. These include:

adorer	*to love*	espérer	*to hope*
aimer	*to like, love*	faillir	*nearly to do something*
aller*	*to go*	il faut	*you must/have to/need to*
compter	*to intend to*	penser	*to intend to*
désirer	*to want, wish*	pouvoir	*to be able to*
détester	*to hate*	préférer	*to prefer to*
devoir	*to have to*	savoir	*to know (how to)*
entendre	*to hear*	vouloir	*to wish, want to*

Example: Je vais sortir   *I shall go out*
           Je voudrais manger   *I'd like to eat*
           Il espère venir   *He hopes to come*
           Je préfère danser   *I prefer dancing*
           Je dois faire mes devoirs   *I have to do my homework*
           Il faut payer   *You have to pay*

French Grammar *Verbs*

Verbs which require à + the infinitive (Des verbes suivis de 'à' et de l'infinitif)

Some common verbs which require **à** before the infinitive include:

aider quelqu'un à	*to help someone to do something*
apprendre à	*to learn to*
commencer à	*to begin to*
consentir à	*to consent to*
continuer à	*to continue to*
se décider* à	*to decide to*
demander à	*to ask to*
hésiter à	*to hesitate to*
inviter quelqu'un à	*to invite someone to do something*
se mettre* à	*to begin to*
obliger quelqu'un à	*to force someone to do something*
passer du temps à	*to spend time in*
réussir à	*to succeed in*

Example:
J'apprends **à** conduire	*I learn/am learning to drive*
Je commence **à** pleurer	*I start crying*
Il consent **à** y aller	*He agrees to go*
Elle continue **à** lire	*She goes on reading*
Je me décide **à** partir	*I make up my mind to go*
Ils demandent **à** sortir	*They ask to go out*
J'hésite **à** y entrer	*I hesitate to go in there*

Verbs which require de + an infinitive (Des verbes suivis de 'de' et de l'infinitif)

Some common verbs which require **de** before the infinitive include:

s'arrêter* de	*to stop doing*
cesser de	*to stop doing*
décider de	*to decide to*
se dépêcher* de	*to hurry to*
dire de	*to tell to*
essayer de	*to try to*
finir de	*to finish*
offrir de	*to offer to*
oublier de	*to forget to*
permettre de	*to allow to*
proposer de	*to suggest*
refuser de	*to refuse to*
regretter de	*to be sorry to*

Example:
Il a cessé de pleuvoir	*It's stopped raining*
Il a décidé de partir	*He decided to leave*
J'ai essayé de te téléphoner	*I tried to phone you*
Elle offre de m'écrire	*She is offering to write to me*
Il propose de partir	*He suggests leaving*
Il refuse de venir	*He refuses to come*

Avoir followed by de + an infinitive (Avoir suivi de 'de' et de l'infinitif)

avoir besoin de	Il a besoin de manger
	He needs food/He needs to eat
avoir le droit de	Nous avons le droit de nous asseoir
	We are allowed to sit down
avoir envie de	J'ai envie de partir
	I want to leave/I feel like leaving
avoir l'intention de	J'ai l'intention de sortir
	I intend to go out
avoir peur de	J'ai peur de sortir la nuit
	I am afraid to go out at night
avoir le temps de	Il a le temps de faire tout ce qu'il veut
	He has the time to do everything he likes

Pour + infinitive (Pour suivi de l'infinitif)

Example: Elle est allée au supermarché pour acheter du sucre
She went to the supermarket to (in order to) buy some sugar
Tu es trop jeune pour conduire
You are too young to drive

Prepositions + infinitive (Des prepositions suivis de l'infinitif)

Sans *without,* **avant de** *before,* **au lieu de** *instead of* are followed by an infinitive:

Example: Elle est sortie **sans** me parler
She went out without speaking to me
Avant de partir, il m'a téléphoné
He rang me before he left
Nous avons décidé de rester **au lieu de** partir
We decided to stay instead of leaving

French Grammar *Verbs*

OTHER SPECIAL CONSTRUCTIONS (D'AUTRES CAS SPÉCIAUX)

1. The verbs **dire, demander, permettre, défendre, conseiller** need **à** with the name of a person followed by **de** with the verb in the infinitive.

    Example: J'ai dit **à** Jean **de** m'écrire   *I told Jean to write to me*

    If the object is a pronoun, use the indirect object pronoun.

    Example: Je **lui** ai dit **de** se dépêcher   *I told him/her to hurry*
    Je **leur** ai demandé **de** sortir   *I asked them to go out*
    Il **me** permet **d'**entrer   *He allows me to go in*
    Elle **lui** défend **de** parler   *She forbids him to speak*
    Je **vous** conseille **de** partir   *I advise you to go*

2. There is no preposition after these verbs in French even though one is needed in English:

    attendre   *to wait for*   écouter   *to listen to*
    chercher   *to look for*   payer   *to pay for*
    craindre   *to be afraid of*   regarder *to look at*
    demander   *to ask for*   sentir   *to smell of*

    Example: J'attends le train   *I wait for the train*
    Je cherche les enfants   *I look for the children*
    Elle craint le danger   *She is afraid of danger*
    Il demande l'addition   *He asks for the bill*
    J'écoute la radio   *I listen to the radio*
    Nous payons les billets   *We pay for the tickets*
    Je regarde les animaux   *I look at the animals*
    Ça sent la lavande   *It smells of lavender*

3. The following verbs need **à** for the person and the word order in French can be different from the word order in English:

    donner quelque chose à quelqu'un
    Je donne de l'argent **à** mon frère
    I give some money to my brother
    I give my brother some money

    envoyer quelque chose à quelqu'un
    Elle envoie une lettre **à** sa sœur
    She sends a letter to her sister
    She sends her sister a letter

85

montrer quelque chose à quelqu'un
Je montre la carte à mon père
I show the map to my father
I show my father the map

prêter quelque chose à quelqu'un
Tu as prêté de l'argent à Paul?
Did you lend some money to Paul?
Did you lend Paul some money?

4. The preposition following the verb in these sentences is also **à**. Here it conveys the idea of *from*.

Il a acheté des pommes à la fermière
He bought the apples from the farmer's wife
Nous avons emprunté la voiture à mon oncle
We borrowed the car from my uncle
Le petit garçon a volé des bonbons à sa sœur
The little boy stole some sweets from his sister

5. Other verbs requiring **à** include:

s'intéresser* à	Je m'intéresse à la musique
	I am interested in music
jouer à	Elle joue **au** tennis
	She plays tennis
pardonner à	Je **lui** pardonne (indirect object pronoun in French)
	I forgive him/her
penser à	Je pense à mon travail/à mes amis
	I'm thinking about my work/my friends
réfléchir à	Elle réfléchissait à la situation
	She was thinking about the situation
ressembler à	Tu ressembles à ton père
	You are like your father
téléphoner à	Je téléphone à ma mère
	I ring my mother

6. Some verbs requiring **de** include:

jouer **de**	Elle joue **de la** guitare
	She plays the guitar
penser **de**	Qu'est-ce que tu penses **de** la maison?
	What do you think of the house?
se souvenir* **de**	Je me souviens **de** mes amis
	I remember my friends

French Grammar *Verbs*

WORD ORDER (L'ORDRE DES MOTS)

Word order in French is fairly similar to English word order, but there are certain differences which you must know:

1. Most **adjectives** come after the noun.
   See pages 9-10.

2. **Adverbs** tend to follow their verb in simple tenses, but often come between the auxiliary and the past participle in compound tenses.
   See page 17.

3. You should take care with the position of the **negatives,** as the word order depends on the negative being used.
   See pages 76-78.

4. **Personal pronouns** are placed before their verb, except when the verb is a positive command.
   See pages 43-44.

5. Remember that **questions** can be asked by inverting the subject and verb.
   See page 79.

6. The verb must always be inverted after **direct speech** (Remember the hyphens).

   Example: "Je ne comprends pas", a-t-il dit
   "I do not understand", he said
   "Je ne crois pas", a-t-elle répondu
   "I don't think so", she answered

7. If the word **peut-être** begins a sentence then the verb and subject are inverted.

   Example: **Peut-être** viendra-t-elle ce soir
   Perhaps she will come this evening

   This can be avoided if the word **que** is added after the word **peut-être** or by placing the **peut-être** later in the sentence.

   Example: **Peut-être qu'**elle viendra ce soir
   Elle viendra ce soir, **peut-être**
   Elle viendra, **peut-être**, ce soir

8. In subordinate clauses introduced by the word **où** the subject and verb must be inverted.

   Example: Voici la maison **où** habitent les Leclerc
   Here is the house where the Leclercs live

REGULAR VERBS

Infinitif/Impératif Infinitive/Imperative	Présent Present	Imparfait Imperfect	Passé Composé Perfect	Futur Future	Passé Simple Past Historic
travailler *to work*	je travaille tu travailles	je travaillais tu travaillais	j'ai travaillé tu as travaillé	je travaillerai tu travailleras	
travaille! travaillons! travaillez!	il/elle travaille nous travaillons vous travaillez ils/elles travaillent	il/elle travaillait nous travaillions vous travailliez ils/elles travaillaient	il/elle a travaillé nous avons travaillé vous avez travaillé ils/elles ont travaillé	il/elle travaillera nous travaillerons vous travaillerez ils/elles travailleront	il/elle travailla ils/elles travaillèrent
finir *to finish*	je finis tu finis	je finissais tu finissais	j'ai fini tu as fini	je finirai tu finiras	
finis! finissons! finissez!	il/elle finit nous finissons vous finissez ils/elles finissent	il/elle finissait nous finissions vous finissiez ils/elles finissaient	il/elle a fini nous avons fini vous avez fini ils/elles ont fini	il/elle finira nous finirons vous finirez ils/elles finiront	il/elle finit ils/elles finirent
ouvrir *to open*	*see irregular verbs*				
répondre *to reply*	je réponds tu réponds	je répondais tu répondais	j'ai répondu tu as répondu	je répondrai tu répondras	
réponds! répondons! répondez!	il/elle répond nous répondons vous répondez ils/elles répondent	il/elle répondait nous répondions vous répondiez ils/elles répondaient	il/elle a répondu nous avons répondu vous avez répondu ils/elles ont répondu	il/elle répondra nous répondrons vous répondrez ils/elles répondront	il/elle répondit ils/elles répondirent

For lists of other regular verbs which follow these patterns, see the following pages:
  -**er** verbs, pages 51-52
  -**er** verbs with slight variations, pages 52-54
  -**ir** verbs, page 54
  -**re** verbs, pages 55-56

French Grammar — *Verb Table*

IRREGULAR VERBS

Infinitif/Impératif Infinitive/Imperative	Présent Present	Imparfait Imperfect	Passé Composé Perfect	Futur Future	Passé Simple Past Historic
accueillir *to welcome*	see cueillir				
aller* *to go* va! (vas-y!) allons! allez!	je vais tu vas il/elle va nous allons vous allez ils/elles vont	j'allais tu allais il/elle allait nous allions vous alliez ils/elles allaient	je suis allé(e) tu es allé(e) il est allé elle est allée vous êtes allé(e)(s) ils sont allés elles sont allées	j'irai tu iras il/elle ira nous irons vous irez ils/elles iront	il/elle alla ils/elles allèrent
(s'*)apercevoir *to notice*	see recevoir				
apparaître *to appear*	see paraître				
appartenir *to belong to*	see tenir				
apprendre *to learn*	see prendre				
s'asseoir* *to sit down* assieds-toi! asseyons-nous! asseyez-vous!	je m'assieds tu t'assieds il/elle s'assied nous nous asseyons vous vous asseyez ils/elles s'asseyent	je m'asseyais tu t'asseyais il/elle s'asseyait nous nous asseyions vous vous asseyiez ils/elles s'asseyaient	je me suis assis(e) tu t'es assis(e) il s'est assis elle s'est assise nous nous sommes assis(es) vous vous êtes assis(e)(es) ils se sont assis elles se sont assises	je m'assiérai tu t'assiéras il/elle s'assiéra nous nous assiérons vous vous assiérez ils/elles s'assiéront	il/elle s'assit ils/elles s'assirent
atteindre *to reach*	see joindre				
avoir *to have* aie! ayons! ayez!	j'ai tu as il/elle a nous avons vous avez ils/elles ont	j'avais tu avais il/elle avait nous avions vous aviez ils/elles avaient	j'ai eu tu as eu il/elle a eu nous avons eu vous avez eu ils/elles ont eu	j'aurai tu auras il/elle aura nous aurons vous aurez ils/elles auront	il/elle eut ils/elles eurent

89

Infinitif/Impératif Infinitive/Imperative	Présent Present	Imparfait Imperfect	Passé Composé Perfect	Futur Future	Passé Simple Past Historic
boire *to drink* bois! buvons! buvez!	je bois tu bois il/elle boit nous buvons vous buvez ils/elles boivent	je buvais tu buvais il/elle buvait nous buvions vous buviez ils/elles buvaient	j'ai bu tu as bu il/elle a bu nous avons bu vous avez bu ils/elles ont bu	je boirai tu boiras il/elle boira nous boirons vous boirez ils/elles boiront	il/elle but ils/elles burent
bouillir *to boil* bous! bouillons! bouillez!	je bous tu bous il/elle bout nous bouillons vous bouillez ils/elles bouillent	je bouillais tu bouillais il/elle bouillait nous bouillions vous bouilliez ils/elles bouillaient	j'ai bouilli tu as bouilli il/elle a bouilli nous avons bouilli vous avez bouilli ils/elles ont bouilli	je bouillirai tu bouilliras il/elle bouillira nous bouillirons vous bouillirez ils/elles bouilliront	il/elle bouillit ils/elles bouillirent
comprendre *to understand*	*see* prendre				
conduire *to drive* conduis! conduisons! conduisez!	je conduis tu conduis il/elle conduit nous conduisons vous conduisez ils/elles conduisent	je conduisais tu conduisais il/elle conduisait nous conduisions vous conduisiez ils/elles conduisaient	j'ai conduit tu as conduit il/elle a conduit nous avons conduit vous avez conduit ils/elles ont conduit	je conduirai tu conduiras il/elle conduira nous conduirons vous conduirez ils/elles conduiront	il/elle conduisit ils/elles conduisirent
connaître *to know* *(a person, place, book, film)* connais! connaissons! connaissez!	je connais tu connais il/elle connaît nous connaissons vous connaissez ils/elles connaissent	je connaissais tu connaissais il/elle connaissait nous connaissions vous connaissiez ils/elles connaissaient	j'ai connu tu as connu il/elle a connu nous avons connu vous avez connu ils/elles ont connu	je connaîtrai tu connaîtras il/elle connaîtra nous connaîtrons vous connaîtrez ils/elles connaîtront	il/elle connut ils/elles connurent

French Grammar   *Verb Table*

Infinitif/Impératif Infinitive/Imperative	Présent Present	Imparfait Imperfect	Passé Composé Perfect	Futur Future	Passé Simple Past Historic
construire *to build* construis! construisons! construisez!	je construis tu construis il/elle construit nous construisons vous construisez ils/elles construisent	je construisais tu construisais il construisait nous construisions vous construisiez ils/elles construisaient	j'ai construit tu as construit il/elle a construit nous avons construit vous avez construit ils/elles ont construit	je construirai tu construiras il/elle construira nous construirons vous construirez ils/elles construiront	il/elle construsit ils/elles construisirent
contenir *to contain*	*see tenir*				
coudre *to sew* couds! cousons! cousez!	je couds tu couds il/elle coud nous cousons vous cousez ils/elles cousent	je cousais tu cousais il/elle cousait nous cousions vous cousiez ils/elles cousaient	j'ai cousu tu as cousu il/elle a cousu nous avons cousu vous avez cousu ils/elles ont cousu	je coudrai tu coudras il/elle coudra nous coudrons vous coudrez ils/elles coudront	il/elle cousit ils/elles cousirent
courir *to run* cours! courons! courez!	je cours tu cours il/elle court nous courons vous courez ils/elles courent	je courais tu courais il/elle courait nous courions vous couriez ils/elles couraient	j'ai couru tu as couru il/elle a couru nous avons couru vous avez couru ils/elles ont couru	je courrai tu courras il/elle courra nous courrons vous courrez ils/elles courront	il/elle courut ils/elles coururent
couvrir *to cover* couvre! couvrons! couvrez!	je couvre tu couvres il/elle couvre nous couvrons vous couvrez ils/elles couvrent	je couvrais tu couvrais il/elle couvrait nous couvrions vous couvriez ils/elles couvraient	j'ai couvert tu as couvert il/elle a couvert nous avons couvert vous avez couvert ils/elles ont couvert	je couvrirai tu couvriras il/elle couvrira nous couvrirons vous couvrirez ils/elles couvriront	il/elle couvrit ils/elles couvrirent

Verb Table — French Grammar

Infinitif/Impératif Infinitive/Imperative	Présent Present	Imparfait Imperfect	Passé Composé Perfect	Futur Future	Passé Simple Past Historic
craindre *to fear, be afraid* crains! craignons! craignez!	je crains tu crains il/elle craint nous craignons vous craignez ils/elles craignent	je craignais tu craignais il/elle craignait nous craignions vous craigniez ils/elles craignaient	j'ai craint tu as craint il/elle a craint nous avons craint vous avez craint ils/elles ont craint	je craindrai tu craindras il/elle craindra nous craindrons vous craindrez ils/elles craindront	il/elle craignit ils/elles craignirent
croire *to believe, think* crois! croyons! croyez!	je crois tu crois il/elle croit nous croyons vous croyez ils/elles croient	je croyais tu croyais il/elle croyait nous croyions vous croyiez ils/elles croyaient	j'ai cru tu as cru il/elle a cru nous avons cru vous avez cru ils/elles ont cru	je croirai tu croiras il/elle croira nous croirons vous croirez ils/elles croiront	il/elle crut ils/elles crurent
cueillir *to pick* cueille! cueillons! cueillez!	je cueille tu cueilles il/elle cueille nous cueillons vous cueillez ils/elles cueillent	je cueillais tu cueillais il/elle cueillait nous cueillions vous cueilliez ils/elles cueillaient	j'ai cueilli tu as cueilli il/elle a cueilli nous avons cueilli vous avez cueilli ils/elles ont cueilli	je cueillerai tu cueilleras il/elle cueillera nous cueillerons vous cueillerez ils/elles cueilleront	il/elle cueillit ils/elles cueillirent
cuire *to cook*	see conduire				
découvrir *to discover*	see couvrir				
décrire *to describe*	see écrire				
détruire *to destroy* détruis! détruisons! détruisez!	je détruis tu détruis il/elle détruit nous détruisons vous détruisez ils/elles détruisent	je détruisais tu détruisais il/elle détruisait nous détruisions vous détruisiez ils/elles détruisaient	j'ai détruit tu as détruit il/elle a détruit nous avons détruit vous avez détruit ils/elles ont détruit	je détruirai tu détruiras il/elle détruira nous détruirons vous détruirez ils/elles détruiront	il/elle détruisit ils/elles détruisirent
devenir* *to become*	see venir*				

French Grammar   *Verb Table*

Infinitif/Impératif Infinitive/Imperative	Présent Present	Imparfait Imperfect	Passé Composé Perfect	Futur Future	Passé Simple Past Historic
devoir *to have to* dois! devons! devez!	je dois tu dois il/elle doit nous devons vous devez ils/elles doivent	je devais tu devais il/elle devait nous devions vous deviez ils/elles devaient	j'ai dû tu as dû il/elle a dû nous avons dû vous avez dû ils/elles ont dû	je devrai tu devras il/elle devra nous devrons vous devrez ils/elles devront	il/elle dut ils/elles durent
dire *to say, tell* dis! disons! dites!	je dis tu dis il/elle dit nous disons vous dites ils/elles disent	je disais tu disais il/elle disait nous disions vous disiez ils/elles disaient	j'ai dit tu as dit il/elle a dit nous avons dit vous avez dit ils/elles ont dit	je dirai tu diras il/elle dira nous dirons vous direz ils/elles diront	il/elle dit ils/elles dirent
dissoudre *to dissolve* dissous! dissolvons! dissolvez!	je dissous tu dissous il/elle dissout nous dissolvons vous dissolvez ils/elles dissolvent	je dissolvais tu dissolvais il/elle dissolvait nous dissolvions vous dissolviez ils/elles dissolvaient	j'ai dissous tu as dissous il/elle a dissous nous avons dissous vous avez dissous ils/elles ont dissous	je dissoudrai tu dissoudras il/elle dissoudra nous dissoudrons vous dissoudrez ils/elles dissoudront	il/elle dissolut ils/elles dissolurent
disparaître *to disappear*	*see* paraître				
dormir *to sleep* dors! dormons! dormez!	je dors tu dors il/elle dort nous dormons vous dormez ils/elles dorment	je dormais tu dormais il/elle dormait nous dormions vous dormiez ils/elles dormaient	j'ai dormi tu as dormi il/elle a dormi nous avons dormi vous avez dormi ils/elles ont dormi	je dormirai tu dormiras il/elle dormira nous dormirons vous dormirez ils/elles dormiront	il/elle dormit ils/elles dormirent

Verb Table — French Grammar

Infinitif/Impératif Infinitive/Imperative	Présent Present	Imparfait Imperfect	Passé Composé Perfect	Futur Future	Passé Simple Past Historic
écrire *to write* écris! écrivons! écrivez!	j'écris tu écris il/elle écrit nous écrivons vous écrivez ils/elles écrivent	j'écrivais tu écrivais il/elle écrivait nous écrivions vous écriviez ils/elles écrivaient	j'ai écrit tu as écrit il/elle a écrit nous avons écrit vous avez écrit ils/elles ont écrit	j'écrirai tu écriras il/elle écrira nous écrirons vous écrirez ils/elles écriront	il/elle écrivit ils/elles écrivirent
s'endormir* *to go to sleep,* *fall asleep* endors-toi! endormons-nous! endormez-vous!	je m'endors tu t'endors il/elle s'endort nous nous endormons vous vous endormez ils/elles s'endorment	je m'endormais tu t'endormais il/elle s'endormait nous nous endormions vous vous endormiez ils/elles s'endormaient	je me suis endormi(e) tu t'es endormi(e) il s'est endormi elle s'est endormie nous nous sommes endormi(e)s vous vous êtes endormi(e)(s) ils se sont endormis elles se sont endormies	je m'endormirai tu t'endormiras il/elle s'endormira nous nous endormirons vous vous endormirez ils/elles s'endormiront	il/elle s'endormit ils/elles s'endormirent
entretenir *to maintain*	see tenir				
éteindre *to extinguish,* *switch off* éteins! éteignons! éteignez!	j'éteins tu éteins il/elle éteint nous éteignons vous éteignez ils/elles éteignent	j'éteignais tu éteignais il/elle éteignait nous éteignions vous éteigniez ils/elles éteignaient	j'ai éteint tu as éteint il/elle a éteint nous avons éteint vous avez éteint ils/elles ont éteint	j'éteindrai tu éteindras il/elle éteindra nous éteindrons vous éteindrez ils/elles éteindront	il/elle éteignit ils/elles éteignirent
être *to be* sois! soyons! soyez!	je suis tu es il/elle est nous sommes vous êtes ils/elles sont	j'étais tu étais il/elle était nous étions vous étiez ils/elles étaient	j'ai été tu as été il/elle a été nous avons été vous avez été ils/elles ont été	je serai tu seras il/elle sera nous serons vous serez ils/elles seront	il/elle fut ils/elles furent

French Grammar — Verb Table

Infinitif/Impératif Infinitive/Imperative	Présent Present	Imparfait Imperfect	Passé Composé Perfect	Futur Future	Passé Simple Past Historic
faire *to do, make*	je fais	je faisais	j'ai fait	je ferai	
	tu fais	tu faisais	tu as fait	tu feras	
fais!	il/elle fait	il/elle faisait	il/elle a fait	il/elle fera	il/elle fit
faisons!	nous faisons	nous faisions	nous avons fait	nous ferons	
faites!	vous faites	vous faisiez	vous avez fait	vous ferez	
	ils/elles font	ils/elles faisaient	ils/elles ont fait	ils/elles feront	ils/elles firent
falloir *to have to*	il faut	il fallait	il a fallu	il faudra	il fallut
fuir *to flee*	je fuis	je fuyais	j'ai fui	je fuirai	
	tu fuis	tu fuyais	tu as fui	tu fuiras	
fuis!	il/elle fuit	il/elle fuyait	il/elle a fui	il/elle fuira	il/elle fuit
fuyons!	nous fuyons	nous fuyions	nous avons fui	nous fuirons	
fuyez!	vous fuyez	vous fuyiez	vous avez fui	vous fuirez	
	ils/elles fuient	ils/elles fuyaient	ils/elles ont fui	ils/elles fuiront	ils/elles fuirent
inscrire *to inscribe*	see écrire				
instruire *to instruct*	see construire				
interdire *to forbid*	see dire				
introduire *to introduce*	see construire				
joindre *to join*	je joins	je joignais	j'ai joint	je joindrai	
	tu joins	tu joignais	tu as joint	tu joindras	
joins!	il/elle joint	il/elle joignait	il/elle a joint	il/elle joindra	il/elle joignit
joignons!	nous joignons	nous joignions	nous avons joint	nous joindrons	
joignez!	vous joignez	vous joigniez	vous avez joint	vous joindrez	
	ils/elles joignent	ils/elles joignaient	ils/elles ont joint	ils/elles joindront	ils/elles joignirent
lire *to read*	je lis	je lisais	j'ai lu	je lirai	
	tu lis	tu lisais	tu as lu	tu liras	
lis!	il/elle lit	il/elle lisait	il/elle a lu	il/elle lira	il/elle lut
lisons!	nous lisons	nous lisions	nous avons lu	nous lirons	
lisez!	vous lisez	vous lisiez	vous avez lu	vous lirez	
	ils/elles lisent	ils/elles lisaient	ils/elles ont lu	ils/elles liront	ils/elles lurent
maintenir *to maintain*	see tenir				

Infinitif/Impératif Infinitive/Imperative	Présent Present	Imparfait Imperfect	Passé Composé Perfect	Futur Future	Passé Simple Past Historic
mentir *to lie* mens! mentons! mentez!	je mens tu mens il/elle ment nous mentons vous mentez ils/elles mentent	je mentais tu mentais il/elle mentait nous mentions vous mentiez ils/elles mentaient	j'ai menti tu as menti il/elle a menti nous avons menti vous avez menti ils/elles ont menti	je mentirai tu mentiras il/elle mentira nous mentirons vous mentirez ils/elles mentiront	il/elle mentit ils/elles mentirent
mettre *to put* mets! mettons! mettez!	je mets tu mets il/elle met nous mettons vous mettez ils/elles mettent	je mettais tu mettais il/elle mettait nous mettions vous mettiez ils/elles mettaient	j'ai mis tu as mis il/elle a mis nous avons mis vous avez mis ils/elles ont mis	je mettrai tu mettras il/elle mettra nous mettrons vous mettrez ils/elles mettront	il/elle mit ils/elles mirent
mourir* *to die* meurs! mourons! mourez!	je meurs tu meurs il/elle meurt nous mourons vous mourez ils/elles meurent	je mourais tu mourais il/elle mourait nous mourions vous mouriez ils/elles mouraient	je suis mort(e) tu es mort(e) il est mort elle est morte nous sommes mort(e)s vous êtes mort(e)(s) ils sont morts elles sont mortes	je mourrai tu mourras il/elle mourra nous mourrons vous mourrez ils/elles mourront	il/elle mourut ils/elles moururent
naître* *to be born* nais! naissons! naissez!	je nais tu nais il/elle naît nous naissons vous naissez ils/elles naissent	je naissais tu naissais il/elle naissait nous naissions vous naissiez ils/elles naissaient	je suis né(e) tu es né(e) il est né elle est née nous sommes né(e)(s) vous êtes né(e)(s) ils sont nés elles sont nées	je naîtrai tu naîtras il/elle naîtra nous naîtrons vous naîtrez ils/elles naîtront	il/elle naquit ils/elles naquirent
obtenir *to obtain*	see tenir				

Infinitif/Impératif Infinitive/Imperative	Présent Present	Imparfait Imperfect	Passé Composé Perfect	Futur Future	Passé Simple Past Historic
offrir *to offer* offre! offrons! offrez!	j'offre tu offres il/elle offre nous offrons vous offrez ils/elles offrent	j'offrais tu offrais il/elle offrait nous offrions vous offriez ils/elles offraient	j'ai offert tu as offert il/elle a offert nous avons offert vous avez offert ils/elles ont offert	j'offrirai tu offriras il/elle offrira nous offrirons vous offrirez ils/elles offriront	il/elle offrit ils/elles offrirent
ouvrir *to open* ouvre! ouvrons! ouvrez!	j'ouvre tu ouvres il/elle ouvre nous ouvrons vous ouvrez ils/elles ouvrent	j'ouvrais tu ouvrais il/elle ouvrait nous ouvrions vous ouvriez ils/elles ouvraient	j'ai ouvert tu as ouvert il/elle a ouvert nous avons ouvert vous avez ouvert ils/elles ont ouvert	j'ouvrirai tu ouvriras il/elle ouvrira nous ouvrirons vous ouvrirez ils/elles ouvriront	il/elle ouvrit ils/elles ouvrirent
paraître *to appear, seem* parais! paraissons! paraissez!	je parais tu parais il/elle paraît nous paraissons vous paraissez ils/elles paraissent	je paraissais tu paraissais il/elle paraissait nous paraissions vous paraissiez ils/elles paraissaient	j'ai paru tu as paru il/elle a paru nous avons paru vous avez paru ils/elles ont paru	je paraîtrai tu paraîtras il/elle paraîtra nous paraîtrons vous paraîtrez ils/elles paraîtront	il/elle parut ils/elles parurent
parcourir *to run along*	*see courir*				
partir* *to leave, go away* pars! partons! partez!	je pars tu pars il/elle part nous partons vous partez ils/elles partent	je partais tu partais il/elle partait nous partions vous partiez ils/elles partaient	je suis parti(e) tu es parti(e) il est parti elle est partie nous sommes parti(e)s vous êtes parti(e)(s) ils sont partis elles sont parties	je partirai tu partiras il/elle partira nous partirons vous partirez ils/elles partiront	il/elle partit ils/elles partirent

Verb Table   **French Grammar**

Infinitif/Impératif Infinitive/Imperative	Présent Present	Imparfait Imperfect	Passé Composé Perfect	Futur Future	Passé Simple Past Historic
parvenir* to manage, get to, reach, succeed parviens! parvenons! parvenez!	je parviens tu parviens il/elle parvient nous parvenons vous parvenez ils/elles parviennent	je parvenais tu parvenais il/elle parvenait nous parvenions vous parveniez ils/elles parvenaient	je suis parvenu(e) tu es parvenu(e) il est parvenu elle est parvenue nous sommes parvenu(e)s vous êtes parvenu(e)(s) ils sont parvenus elles sont parvenues	je parviendrai tu parviendras il/elle parviendra nous parviendrons vous parviendrez ils/elles parviendront	il/elle parvint ils/elle parvinrent
peindre to paint peins! peignons! peignez!	je peins tu peins il/elle peint nous peignons vous peignez ils/elles peignent	je peignais tu peignais il/elle peignait nous peignions vous peigniez ils/elles peignaient	j'ai peint tu as peint il/elle a peint nous avons peint vous avez peint ils/elles ont peint	je peindrai tu peindras il/elle peindra nous peindrons vous peindrez ils/elles peindront	il/elle peignit ils/elles peignirent
permettre to permit	see mettre				
se plaindre* to complain plains-toi! plaignons-nous! plaignez-vous!	je me plains tu te plains il/elle se plaint nous nous plaignons vous vous plaignez ils/elles se plaignent	je me plaignais tu te plaignais il/elle se plaignait nous nous plaignions vous vous plaigniez ils/elles se plaignaient	je me suis plaint(e) tu t'es plaint(e) il s'est plaint elle s'est plainte nous nous sommes plaint(e)s vous vous êtes plaint(e)(s) ils se sont plaints elles se sont plaintes	je me plaindrai tu te plaindras il/elle se plaindra nous nous plaindrons vous vous plaindrez ils/elles se plaindront	il/elle se plaignit ils/elles se plaignirent
plaire to please plais! plaisons! plaisez!	je plais tu plais il/elle plaît nous plaisons vous plaisez ils/elles plaisent	je plaisais tu plaisais il/elle plaisait nous plaisions vous plaisiez ils/elles plaisaient	j'ai plu tu as plu il/elle a plu nous avons plu vous avez plu ils/elles ont plu	je plairai tu plairas il/elle plaira nous plairons vous plairez ils/elles plairont	il/elle plut ils/elles plurent
pleuvoir to rain	il pleut	il pleuvait	il a plu	il pleuvra	il plut

French Grammar   *Verb Table*

Infinitif/Impératif Infinitive/Imperative	Présent Present	Imparfait Imperfect	Passé Composé Perfect	Futur Future	Passé Simple Past Historic
poursuivre *to pursue*	*see* suivre				
pouvoir *to be able to, can*	je peux (puis-je?) tu peux il/elle peut nous pouvons vous pouvez ils/elles peuvent	je pouvais tu pouvais il/elle pouvait nous pouvions vous pouviez ils/elles pouvaient	j'ai pu tu as pu il/elle a pu nous avons pu vous avez pu ils/elles ont pu	je pourrai tu pourras il/elle pourra nous pourrons vous pourrez ils/elles pourront	il/elle put ils/elles purent
prendre *to take* prends! prenons! prenez!	je prends tu prends il/elle prend nous prenons vous prenez ils/elles prennent	je prenais tu prenais il/elle prenait nous prenions vous preniez ils/elles prenaient	j'ai pris tu as pris il/elle a pris nous avons pris vous avez pris ils/elles ont pris	je prendrai tu prendras il/elle prendra nous prendrons vous prendrez ils/elles prendront	il/elle prit ils/elle prirent
prescrire *to prescribe*	*see* écrire				
prévenir *to warn, inform* préviens! prévenons! prévenez!	je préviens tu préviens il/elle prévient nous prévenons vous prévenez ils/elles préviennent	je prévenais tu prévenais il/elle prévenait nous prévenions vous préveniez ils/elles prévenaient	j'ai prévenu tu as prévenu il/elle a prévenu nous avons prévenu vous avez prévenu ils/elles ont prévenu	je préviendrai tu préviendras il/elle préviendra nous préviendrons vous préviendrez ils/elles préviendront	il/elle prévint ils/elles prévinrent
prévoir *to foresee*	*see* voir				
produire *to produce*	*see* construire				
promettre *to promise*	*see* mettre				

99

Verb Table — French Grammar

Infinitif/Impératif Infinitive/Imperative	Présent Present	Imparfait Imperfect	Passé Composé Perfect	Futur Future	Passé Simple Past Historic
recevoir *to receive*	je reçois	je recevais	j'ai reçu	je recevrai	
	tu reçois	tu recevais	tu as reçu	tu recevras	
reçois!	il/elle reçoit	il/elle recevait	il/elle a reçu	il/elle recevra	il/elle reçut
recevons!	nous recevons	nous recevions	nous avons reçu	nous recevrons	
recevez!	vous recevez	vous receviez	vous avez reçu	vous recevrez	
	ils/elles reçoivent	ils/elles recevaient	ils/elles ont reçu	ils/elles recevront	ils/elles reçurent
reconnaître *to recognise*	je reconnais	je reconnaissais	j'ai reconnu	je reconnaîtrai	
	tu reconnais	tu reconnaissais	tu as reconnu	tu reconnaîtras	
reconnais!	il/elle reconnaît	il/elle reconnaissait	il/elle a reconnu	il/elle reconnaîtra	il/elle reconnut
reconnaissons!	nous reconnaissons	nous reconnaissions	nous avons reconnu	nous reconnaîtrons	
reconnaissez!	vous reconnaissez	vous reconnaissiez	vous avez reconnu	vous reconnaîtrez	ils/elles
	ils/elles reconnaissent	ils/elles reconnaissaient	ils/elles ont reconnu	ils/elles reconnaîtront	reconnurent
recouvrir *to cover, recover*	*see* couvrir				
réduire *to reduce*	je réduis	je réduisais	j'ai réduit	je réduirai	
	tu réduis	tu réduisais	tu as réduit	tu réduiras	
réduis!	il/elle réduit	il/elle réduisait	il/elle a réduit	il/elle réduira	il/elle réduit
réduisons!	nous réduisons	nous réduisions	nous avons réduit	nous réduirons	
réduisez!	vous réduisez	vous réduisiez	vous avez réduit	vous réduirez	
	ils/elles réduisent	ils/elles réduisaient	ils/elles ont réduit	ils/elles réduiront	ils/elles réduirent
refaire *to re-do, re-make*	*see* faire				
rejoindre *to re-join*	*see* joindre				
relire *to re-read*	*see* lire				
reluire *to shine*	*see* conduire				
remettre *to put back*	*see* mettre				
repartir* *to leave again*	*see* partir*				

French Grammar *Verb Table*

Infinitif/Impératif Infinitive/Imperative	Présent Present	Imparfait Imperfect	Passé Composé Perfect	Futur Future	Passé Simple Past Historic
reprendre *to take, resume, get back*	see prendre				
résoudre *to solve* résous! résolvons! résolvez!	je résous tu résous il/elle résout nous résolvons vous résolvez ils/elles résolvent	je résolvais tu résolvais il/elle résolvait nous résolvions vous résolviez ils/elles résolvaient	j'ai résolu tu as résolu il/elle a résolu nous avons résolu vous avez résolu ils/elles ont résolu	je résoudrai tu résoudras il/elle résoudra nous résoudrons vous résoudrez ils/elles résoudront	il/elle résolut ils/elles résolurent
ressentir *to feel, experience*	see sentir				
retenir *to hold back, keep*	see tenir				
revenir* *to come back return*	see venir*				
revoir *to see again*	see voir				
rire *to laugh* ris! rions! riez!	je ris tu ris il/elle rit nous rions vous riez ils/elles rient	je riais tu riais il/elle riait nous riions vous riiez ils/elles riaient	j'ai ri tu as ri il/elle a ri nous avons ri vous avez ri ils/elles ont ri	je rirai tu riras il/elle rira nous rirons vous rirez ils/elles riront	il/elle rit ils/elles rirent
satisfaire *to satisfy*	see faire				
savoir *to know (a fact, or how to do something)* sache! sachons! sachez!	je sais tu sais il/elle sait nous savons vous savez ils/elles savent	je savais tu savais il/elle savait nous savions vous saviez ils/elles savaient	j'ai su tu as su il/elle a su nous avons su vous avez su ils/elles ont su	je saurai tu sauras il/elle saura nous saurons vous saurez ils/elles sauront	il/elle sut ils surent

Verb Table — French Grammar

Infinitif/Impératif Infinitive/Imperative	Présent Present	Imparfait Imperfect	Passé Composé Perfect	Futur Future	Passé Simple Past Historic
sentir *to smell,* *feel, sense* sens! sentons! sentez!	je sens tu sens il/elle sent nous sentons vous sentez ils/elles sentent	je sentais tu sentais il/elle sentait nous sentions vous sentiez ils/elles sentaient	j'ai senti tu as senti il/elle a senti nous avons senti vous avez senti ils/elles ont senti	je sentirai tu sentiras il/elle sentira nous sentirons vous sentirez ils/elles sentiront	il/elle sentit ils/elles sentirent
se sentir* *to feel,* *(ill well, etc)* sens-toi! sentons-nous! sentez-vous!	je me sens tu te sens il/elle se sent nous nous sentons vous vous sentez ils/elles se sentent	je me sentais tu te sentais il/elle se sentait nous nous sentions vous vous sentiez ils/elles se sentaient	je me suis senti(e) tu t'es senti(e) il s'est senti elle s'est sentie nous nous sommes senti(e)s vous vous êtes senti(e)(s) ils se sont sentis elles se sont senties	je me sentirai tu te sentiras il/elle se sentira nous nous sentirons vous vous sentirez ils/elles se sentiront	il/elle se sentit ils/elles se sentirent
servir *to serve* sers! servons! servez!	je sers tu sers il/elle sert nous servons vous servez ils/elles servent	je servais tu servais il/elle servait nous servions vous serviez ils/elles servaient	j'ai servi tu as servi il/elle a servi nous avons servi vous avez servi ils/elles ont servi	je servirai tu serviras il/elle servira nous servirons vous servirez ils/elles serviront	il/elle servit ils/elles servirent
se servir* (de) *to use* sers-toi! servons-nous! servez-vous!	je me sers tu te sers il/elle se sert nous nous servons vous vous servez ils/elles se servent	je me servais tu te servais il/elle se servait nous nous servions vous vous serviez ils/elles se servaient	je me suis servi(e) tu t'es servi(e) il s'est servi elle s'est servie nous nous sommes servi(e)s vous vous êtes servi(e)(s) ils se sont servis elles se sont servies	je me servirai tu te serviras il/elle se servira nous nous servirons vous vous servirez ils/elles se serviront	il/elle se servit ils/elles se servirent

French Grammar — *Verb Table*

Infinitif/Impératif Infinitive/Imperative	Présent Present	Imparfait Imperfect	Passé Composé Perfect	Futur Future	Passé Simple Past Historic
sortir* *to go out* sors! sortons! sortez!	je sors tu sors il/elle sort nous sortons vous sortez ils/elles sortent	je sortais tu sortais il/elle sortait nous sortions vous sortiez ils/elles sortaient	je suis sorti(e) ‡ tu es sorti(e) il est sorti elle est sortie nous sommes sorti(e)s vous êtes sorti(e)(s) ils sont sortis elles sont sorties	je sortirai tu sortiras il/elle sortira nous sortirons vous sortirez ils/elles sortiront	il/elle sortit ils/elles sortirent
souffrir *to suffer* souffre! souffrons! souffrez!	je souffre tu souffres il/elle souffre nous souffrons vous souffrez ils/elles souffrent	je souffrais tu souffrais il/elle souffrait nous souffrions vous souffriez ils/elles souffraient	j'ai souffert tu as souffert il/elle a souffert nous avons souffert vous avez souffert ils/elles ont souffert	je souffrirai tu souffriras il/elle souffrira nous souffrirons vous souffrirez ils/elles souffriront	il/elle souffrit ils/elles souffrirent
soumettre *to submit*	*see* mettre				
sourire *to smile* souris! sourions! souriez!	je souris tu souris il/elle sourit nous sourions vous souriez ils/elles sourient	je souriais tu souriais il/elle souriait nous sourions vous souriez ils/elles souriaient	j'ai souri tu as souri il/elle a souri nous avons souri vous avez souri ils/elles ont souri	je sourirai tu souriras il/elle sourira nous sourirons vous sourirez ils/elles souriront	il/elle sourit ils/elles sourirent
soutenir *to support*	*see* tenir				
se souvenir* de *to remember*	*see* venir*				

‡ *use* avoir *as the auxiliary if there is a direct object, e.g.* j'ai sorti mon mouchoir

103

Verb Table — French Grammar

Infinitif/Impératif Infinitive/Imperative	Présent Present	Imparfait Imperfect	Passé Composé Perfect	Futur Future	Passé Simple Past Historic
suffire *to suffice* suffis! suffisons! suffisez!	je suffis tu suffis il/elle suffit nous suffisons vous suffisez ils/elles suffisent	je suffisais tu suffisais il/elle suffisait nous suffisions vous suffisiez ils/elles suffisaient	j'ai suffi tu as suffi il/elle a suffi nous avons suffi vous avez suffi ils/elles ont suffi	je suffirai tu suffiras il/elle suffira nous suffirons vous suffirez ils/elles suffiront	il/elle suffit ils/elles suffirent
suivre *to follow* suis! suivons! suivez!	je suis tu suis il/elle suit nous suivons vous suivez ils/elles suivent	je suivais tu suivais il/elle suivait nous suivions vous suiviez ils/elles suivaient	j'ai suivi tu as suivi il/elle a suivi nous avons suivi vous avez suivi ils/elles ont suivi	je suivrai tu suivras il/elle suivra nous suivrons vous suivrez ils/elles suivront	il/elle suivit ils/elles suivirent
surprendre *to surprise*	see prendre				
survenir* *to take place*	see venir*				
survivre *to survive*	see vivre				
se taire* *to be silent* tais-toi! taisons-nous! taisez -vous!	je me tais tu te tais il/elle se tait nous nous taisons vous vous taisez ils/elles se taisent	je me taisais tu te taisais il/elle se taisait nous nous taisions vous vous taisiez ils/elles se taisaient	je me suis tu(e) tu t'es tu(e) il s'est tu elle s'est tu(e) nous nous sommes tu(e)s vous vous êtes tu(e)(s) ils se sont tus elle se sont tues	je me tairai tu te tairas il/elle se taira nous nous tairons vous vous tairez ils/elles se tairont	il/elle se tut ils/elles se turent
tenir *to hold* tiens! tenons! tenez!	je tiens tu tiens il/elle tient nous tenons vous tenez ils/elles tiennent	je tenais tu tenais il/elle tenait nous tenions vous teniez ils/elles tenaient	j'ai tenu tu as tenu il/elle a tenu nous avons tenu vous avez tenu ils/elles ont tenu	je tiendrai tu tiendras il/elle tiendra nous tiendrons vous tiendrez ils/elles tiendront	il/elle tint ils/elles tinrent

French Grammar — *Verb Table*

Infinitif/Impératif Infinitive/Imperative	Présent Present	Imparfait Imperfect	Passé Composé Perfect	Futur Future	Passé Simple Past Historic
se tenir* *to stand* tiens-toi! tenons-nous! tenez-vous!	je me tiens tu te tiens il/elle se tient nous nous tenons vous vous tenez ils/elles se tiennent	je me tenais tu te tenais il/elle se tenait nous nous tenions vous vous teniez ils/elles se tenaient	je me suis tenu(e) tu t'es tenu(e) il s'est tenu elle s'est tenue nous nous sommes tenu(e)s vous vous êtes tenu(e)(s) ils se sont tenus elles se sont tenues	je me tiendrai tu te tiendras il/elle se tiendra nous nous tiendrons vous vous tiendrez ils/elles se tiendront	il/elle se tint ils/elles se tinrent
traduire *to translate*	see conduire				
transmettre *to transmit*	see mettre				
vaincre *to defeat* vaincs! vainquons vainquez!	je vaincs tu vaincs il/elle vainc nous vainquons vous vainquez ils/elles vainquent	je vainquais tu vainquais il/elle vainquait nous vainquions vous vainquiez ils/elles vainquaient	j'ai vaincu tu as vaincu il/elle a vaincu nous avons vaincu vous avez vaincu ils/elles ont vaincu	je vaincrai tu vaincras il/elle vaincra nous vaincrons vous vaincrez ils/elles vaincront	il/elle vainquit ils/elles vainquirent
valoir *to be worth*	je vaux tu vaux il/elle vaut nous valons vous valez ils/elles valent	je valais tu valais il/elle valait nous valions vous valiez ils/elles valaient	j'ai valu tu as valu il/elle a valu nous avons valu vous avez valu ils/elles ont valu	je vaudrai tu vaudras il/elle vaudra nous vaudrons vous vaudrez ils/elles vaudront	il/elle valut ils/elles valurent

Verb Table   **French Grammar**

Infinitif/Impératif Infinitive/Imperative	Présent Present	Imparfait Imperfect	Passé Composé Perfect	Futur Future	Passé Simple Past Historic
venir* *to come* viens! venons! venez!	je viens tu viens il/elle vient nous venons vous venez ils/elles viennent	je venais tu venais il/elle venait nous venions vous veniez ils/elles venaient	je suis venu(e) tu es venu(e) il est venu elle est venue nous sommes venu(e)s vous êtes venu(e)(s) ils sont venus elles sont venues	je viendrai tu viendras il/elle viendra nous viendrons vous viendrez ils/elles viendront	il/elle vint ils/elles vinrent
vivre *to live, be alive* vis! vivons! vivez!	je vis tu vis il/elle vit nous vivons vous vivez ils/elles vivent	je vivais tu vivais il/elle vivait nous vivions vous viviez ils/elles vivaient	j'ai vécu tu as vécu il/elle a vécu nous avons vécu vous avez vécu ils/elles ont vécu	je vivrai tu vivras il/elle vivra nous vivrons vous vivrez ils/elles vivront	il/elle vécut ils/elles vécurent
voir *to see* vois! voyons! voyez!	je vois tu vois il/elle voit nous voyons vous voyez ils/elles voient	je voyais tu voyais il/elle voyait nous voyions vous voyiez ils/elles voyaient	j'ai vu tu as vu il/elle a vu nous avons vu vous avez vu ils/elles ont vu	je verrai tu verras il/elle verra nous verrons vous verrez ils/elles verront	il/elle vit ils elles virent
vouloir *to wish, want* veuille! veuillons! veuillez!	je veux tu veux il/elle veut nous voulons vous voulez ils/elles veulent	je voulais tu voulais il/elle voulait nous voulions vous vouliez ils/elles voulaient	j'ai voulu tu as voulu il/elle a voulu nous avons voulu vous avez voulu ils/elles ont voulu	je voudrai tu voudras il/elle voudra nous voudrons vous voudrez ils/elles voudront	il/elle voulut ils/elles voulurent

If you are looking for a reflexive verb and do not find it in the table, look for it without se or s'
Example: se mettre* en colère   *see* mettre
Do remember that all reflexive verbs take être in the Perfect Tense even when the non-reflexive verb takes avoir!

Index

à 36
abstract nouns 2
active voice 5, 74
adjectives 1, 6-10
adjectives with two meanings 10
adverbs 1, 16-19
ago 35
agreement of adjectives 1, 6
agreement of past participle 60
articles 1, 20-23
au, aux 21
auquel 46
aussi ... que 11, 18
avoidance of the passive 74
avoir + *de* + infinitive 84
beau 7
beaucoup 18, 19
bien 18, 19
cardinal numbers 32
chaque 15
clause 1
collective nouns 31
commands 5, 75
common adverbs 19
common nouns 2
common reflexive verbs 57
common regular **-er** verbs 52
common regular **-ir** verbs 54-55
common regular **-re** verbs 56
comparison of adjectives 1, 11
comparison of adverbs 1, 18
compound nouns 30
concrete nouns 2
conditional tense 70
conjugation 4
conjunctions 2, 24
conseiller 85
dates 34
days of the week 34
de 22-23
défendre 85
definite article 1, 20
demander 85
demonstrative adjectives 14
demonstrative pronouns 2, 48
depuis 51, 57
devoir 80
dire 85
direct object pronouns 2, 42

disjunctive pronouns 44
du, des 21-22
duquel 46
emphatic pronouns 2, 44
en 38, 42, 67
en train de 58
être as an auxiliary verb 60
être in the imperfect tense 64
être sur le point de 58
feminine 25
feminine forms of masculine nouns ...27-28
feminine of adjectives 6-8
feminine of nouns 25, 27-28
festivals 34
for 35
formation of adverbs 16
fou 7
future tense 68-70
future tense with *aller* 68
gender 2, 25-28
il y a 51
immediate future tense 68
imperative 5, 75
imperfect tense 63-65
in 35
indefinite adjectives 15
indefinite article 1, 21
indefinite pronouns 3, 50
indirect object pronouns 3, 42
infinitive 4, 82
interrogative adjectives 14
interrogative pronouns 3, 47
invariable adjectives 8
irregular adjectives 8
irregular **-er** verbs 52
irregular future tense forms 70
irregular imperative forms 75
irregular **-ir** verbs 55
irregular **-re** verbs 56, 89-106
irregular verbs 4, 89-106
irregular verbs with *avoir* in the perfect .. 59
le moins 12, 18
le plus 12, 18
le, la 25
lequel 46
masculine 25-26
meilleur 12
mille 32
modal verbs 80-82

Index

French Grammar

moindre 11-12
moins ... que 11, 18
months 34
more adjectives 13
more adverbs 19
mou 7
negatives 76-78
noun plurals with irregularities 30-31
nouns 2, 25-31
nouveau 7
number 2
numbers, times and dates 32-35
numbers 32
object 4
omission of the article 21-22
order of pronouns 44
ordinal numbers 33
partitive article 1, 22-23
passive voice 5, 74
past historic 71-73
past participles 5, 58-60
PDO (preceding direct object) 60
perfect infinitive 62
perfect tense 58-62
perfect tense of reflexive verbs 61-62
perfect tense with *avoir* 58-60
perfect tense with *être* 60
permettre 85
personal pronouns 3, 41
peut-être 87
pire 11-12
pluperfect tense 65-66
plural of adjectives 6-8
plural of nouns 2, 29
plus ... que 11, 18
position of adjectives 9
position of adverbs 17
position of pronouns 43
possessive adjectives 13
possessive case 31
possessive pronouns 3, 49
pour + infinitive 84
pouvoir 81
preceding direct object (PDO) 60
prepositions 2, 36-40
prepositions + infinitive 84
present tense of **-er** verbs 51, 88
present tense of **-ir** verbs 54, 88
present tense of **-oir** verbs 56, 89-106
present tense of **-re** verbs 55, 88
present tense of reflexive verbs 56
present participle 5, 66-67

present participle of *avoir* 67
present participle of *être* 67
present tense 51-58
present tense constructions 57
pronouns 2, 41-50
proper nouns 2
quelque 15
question words 79
questions 79
reflexive pronouns 3, 56-57
reflexive verbs 4, 56, 61-62
reflexive verbs in the perfect tense 61-62
regular **-er** verbs with variations .. 52-54, 65
regular verb table 88
relative pronouns 3, 45
savoir 81
singular of adjectives 6-9
singular of nouns 2, 25-28
special days 34
stressed pronouns 44
subject 5
subject pronouns 3, 41
superlative 1, 12
superlative of adjectives 12
superlative of adverbs 18
tel 15
times 33, 35
two genders, two meanings 28
un, une 25
venir de 58
verb table 88-106
verb tenses 5, 51-74
verbal constructions 85
verbs 3, 51-87
verbs + *à* 83, 86
verbs + *de* 83-84, 86
verbs + infinitive only 82
verbs without a preposition in French 85
vieux 7
voilà 51
vouloir 82
word order 87
word order with negatives 76-78
y 42

108